25 WALKS

HIGHLAND PERTHSHIRE

Roger Smith

Series Editor: Roger Smith

Second Edition

mercatpress
www.mercatpress.com

First published 1994

This edition published in 2002 by Mercat Press

Mercat Press Ltd., 10 Coates Crescent, Edinburgh EH1 2EL

2 303904 21   © Mercat Press 2002

ISBN: 184183 0356

Acknowledgements

A number of people have helped greatly with the compilation of this book. I would especially like to thank John Dunn, former Senior Countryside Ranger with Perth & Kinross Council, for very helpful advice. The Council have done great things in opening up and extending the network of walks available in the area.

I would also like to thank Chris Ford and Syd House of Forest Enterprise; Polly Freeman, ranger for the Atholl Estates; and Seán Costello and Tom Johnstone of Mercat Press for continued encouragement and support.

Perthshire Tourist Board and Ian Reynolds are thanked for their help in supplying photographs. Other photographs are by the author.

Roger Smith, July 2002.

CONTENTS

Useful Information.. vi

Introduction.. vii

Walk 1 – The Pass of Killiecrankie........................ 1

Walk 2 – Around Loch Faskally............................. 5

Walk 3 – KIlliecrankie and Tenandry....................... 9

Walk 4 – Killiecrankie Reserve........................... 15

Walk 5 – Ben Vrackie..................................... 19

Walk 6 – Craigower....................................... 23

Walk 7 – The Black Spout and Edradour.................... 27

Walk 8 – Moors and Megaliths............................. 31

Walk 9 – Rob Roy and the Picts........................... 37

Walk 10 – Allean Forest.................................. 41

Walk 11 – Historic Dunkeld and Birnam.................... 45

Walk 12 – The Braan and Rumbling Bridge.................. 49

Walk 13 – Birnam Hill.................................... 55

Walk 14 – The Larch Walk................................. 59

Walk 15 – Mill Dam....................................... 63

Walk 16 – The Banks o' Tay............................... 67

Walk 17 – Fungarth and Loch of the Lowes................. 71

Walk 18 – Dunkeld to Ballinluig.......................... 75

Walk 19 – The Birks of Aberfeldy......................... 79

Walk 20 – Weem Woods and Castle Menzies.................. 83

Walk 21 – Castle Dow..................................... 89

Walk 22 – Drummond Hill.................................. 93

Walk 23 – The Falls of Acharn............................ 97

Walk 24 – Glen Tilt..................................... 101

Walk 25 – The Falls of Bruar............................ 105

Index 109

USEFUL INFORMATION

The length of each walk is given in kilometres and miles, but within the text measurements are metric for simplicity. The walks are described in detail and have accompanying maps (study these before you set out) so there should be little chance of getting lost. If you do want a back-up, you will find Ordnance Survey maps on sale locally.

Every care has been taken to make the descriptions and maps as accurate as possible, but the author and publishers can accept no responsibility for errors, however caused. The countryside is always changing and there will inevitably be alterations to some aspects of these walks as time goes by. The publishers and author are happy to receive comments and suggested amendments for future editions.

Tourist Information

For general information on the area, accommodation enquiries etc, contact the Perthshire Tourist Board, Lower City Mills, West Mill Street, Perth PH1 5QP, phone 01738 450600, or visit their website at *www.perthshire.co.uk*.

There are three Tourist Information Centres in the area covered by the book; all offer a wide range of helpful services and are open all year. They are at:

The Square, Aberfeldy PH15 2DD

t. 01887 820276

The Cross, Dunkeld PH8 OAN

t. 01350 727688

22 Atholl Road, Pitlochry PH16 5BX

t. 01796 472215/472751

METRIC MEASUREMENTS

At the beginning of each walk, the distance is given in miles and kilometres. Within the text, all measurements are metric for simplicity (OS maps are also now all metric). However, a conversion table might still be useful.

The basic statistic to remember is that one kilometre is five-eighths of a mile. Half a mile is equivalent to 800 metres and a quarter-mile is 400 metres. Below that distance, yards and metres are little different in practical terms.

km	miles
1	0.625
1.6	1
2	1.25
3	1.875
3.2	2
4	2.5
4.8	3
5	3.125
6	3.75
6.4	4
7	4.375
8	5
9	5.625
10	6.25
16	10

Abbreviations

You may find the following abbreviations used in the text.

NTS: The National Trust for Scotland. NTS has in its care over 100 properties of all kinds, ranging from small vernacular cottages and individual landscape features to great houses and large areas of superb mountain country. *www.nts.org.uk*.

OS: Ordnance Survey. The OS is our national mapping agency, covering the whole of the UK at various scales. The two scales most frequently used by walkers are 1:25,000 (Explorer maps) and 1:50,000 (Landranger maps). All OS maps are drawn on a grid of kilometre squares. *www.ordsvy.gov.uk*.

RSPB: Royal Society for the Protection of Birds. The largest conservation body of its kind in the UK. *www.rspb.org.uk*.

SNH: Scottish Natural Heritage. The government conservation agency in Scotland. Formed in 1992 by a merger of the former Nature Conservancy Council and the Countryside Commission for Scotland, SNH has a remit covering scientific research, habitat conservation, access and recreation. *www.snh.gov.uk*.

Walking in Highland Perthshire

INTRODUCTION

This book describes 25 walks in a roughly triangular area with Blair Atholl, Kenmore and Dunkeld as its three corners. It is an area rightly famed for its varied and beautiful scenery, and also has many fascinating historical connections. The walks visit ancient stone circles and burial mounds, mysterious Pictish stones, historic castles, a major battle site and many other equally interesting places. The wildlife is also rich.

In compiling the book, I have tried to keep in mind the visitor who enjoys a walk rather than the hardened hillwalker who wishes to bag half a dozen tops in a day. Most of the walks are 4–8 miles (7–14km) in length, and are well within the compass of any reasonably fit person. Most are on good paths and tracks. There is one genuine hillwalk (Ben Vrackie), on a well-used path that leads to a summit with a superb panoramic view. Try to keep a good day aside for that one if you can.

The weather in this part of Scotland is inevitably variable, but Perthshire is drier than the west, and you will be very unlucky not to have some sunshine during your stay. April to June are often the driest months, with July and August rather damper. However, there are compensations for that as several of the walks visit very fine waterfalls which are at their best after periods of rain.

Generally speaking, sophisticated protective clothing should not be needed apart from the hillwalk mentioned above, when it is essential to carry good waterproofs. Information at the beginning of each walk indicates whether strong footwear such as boots is advised: in some cases the walks can be completed in trainers without any difficulty.

Some of the walks are wholly or partly on roads, but apart from a short section on the Castle Menzies walk out of Aberfeldy, the roads used are very quiet and carry little traffic. Care is nonetheless advised, and the rule is, if there is no pavement, walk in single file facing the traffic (i.e. on the right of the road).

The walk descriptions, and the accompanying maps, should be sufficiently detailed to avoid the possibility of getting lost; many of the walks are waymarked too. However, if you like a back-up then I recommend the 1: 50,000 Ordnance Survey Landranger maps, which are on sale locally. The new 1:25,000 Explorer series was due to reach this area during 2002, and would be even better.

The walks should nearly all be suitable for families, and most can easily be completed by all but the youngest children. If you take a dog, please ensure that it is under close control. Dogs should be kept on a lead when crossing farmland, and during the lambing period (March to May in this part of Scotland) you are asked not to take dogs through fields of sheep. Many of the walks do not cross farmland so dogs can still be taken on them even in this sensitive period.

If you complete all these walks, you will have got to know the area and its delights quite well. I hope those you do complete will be enjoyable and will whet your appetite for further visits and perhaps longer excursions. Even though I am fortunate enough to know the area well, I never tire of exploring it on foot—by far the best way—and I am always coming across new views, hidden corners and previously undiscovered historical connections.

The book has been thoroughly revised and several new walks included for this second edition. I hope it is your companion on many pleasurable excursions into the delightful countryside of Highland Perthshire.

Roger Smith

Taymouth Castle and golf course

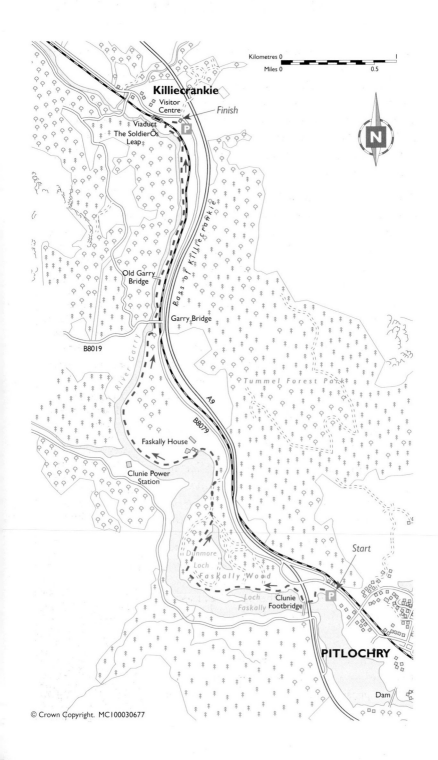

© Crown Copyright. MC100030677

THE PASS OF KILLIECRANKIE

Killiecrankie is famous for the 1689 battle but the gorge is also a superb natural site with a fine river, lovely trees and a good range of wildlife. This out-and-back route is a lovely walk at any time of year, but as with many walks in this area, it is perhaps particularly fine in the autumn, when the colouring on the trees is quite spectacular.

From the car park, where there is a small café and shop, follow the signposts and walk beside Loch Faskally to pass under the bridge carrying the A9. The bridge, constructed by Balfour Beatty, won a Saltire Society award for its design. Beside it is the Clunie footbridge. Loch Faskally was artificially created as part of a major hydro-electric scheme, but now appears as a natural part of the scene.

Continue into Faskally Wood by a zigzag path up steps, following white markers on posts. The path winds through the wood, which has a good variety of trees and is often rich in birdsong, with the traffic noise from the A9 gradually diminishing as you walk. Don't be confused by green waymarks – continue following the tall round posts. There is a surprising amount of up and down on this section. After about 1km the path goes downhill to pass the very attractive Dunmore Loch: reedy, covered in water-lilies and a riot of colour in season.

Past the loch, turn left on a minor road which leads to the Freshwater Fisheries Research Station. Before reaching the laboratories, turn left to walk back to the lochside around the grounds of Faskally House, an outdoor centre for young people, run by a charity.

The walk now continues beside the River Garry as it empties into the loch, with the Clunie Power Station opposite. The Garry is a spate river, and in flood rises very rapidly. When it is low, extensive

INFORMATION

Distance: 6km (3.5 miles) one way or 12km (7 miles) return.

Start and finish: Clunie car park, reached by taking the B8019 road north of Pitlochry and turning off a mile north of the town following Tay Forest Park signs.

Terrain: Good tracks and paths. No special footwear needed.

Refreshments: Café at start, and at the National Trust for Scotland Visitor Centre at Killiecrankie (both open April-October).

Toilets: At the Visitor Centre.

Opening hours: NTS Visitor Centre at Killiecrankie: 1 Apr-31 Oct daily, 1000-1730. Admission charge for non-members. Rangers regularly lead walks—details at the Centre or from the Tourist Information Centre in Pitlochry.

KIlliecrankie Gorge

Soldier's Leap

shingle banks are revealed. Its name comes from the Gaelic *garbh*, meaning 'rough'. The Pass of Killiecrankie is now clearly visible ahead, and in the distance, half right, is the bulk of Carn Liath ('the grey hill', and well named).

At the end of the fields, turn right, then left down steps to cross a burn. After 600m, pass under the Garry Bridge, which carries the B8019 high overhead, and walk into the gorge. This was the only route through the Pass until the railway and the successive modern roads were made. The latest of these is high above to the right, on a viaduct as it cuts directly across the hillslope.

The path passes the old Garry Bridge, now a footbridge. Just beyond it, where the path forks left, an old milestone on the right says you are 11 miles from Tummel Bridge and 3 from Blair Atholl. The path passes the Balfour Stone, where Brigadier Barthold Balfour of the Dutch Brigade, commander of the left wing of General Mackay's army, was killed in the 1689 battle. The full story of the battle is told at the NTS Visitor Centre, towards which you are now heading. The centre also has displays on the wildlife and geology of the area.

In summary, the battle, between government forces under Mackay and Jacobite rebels under John Graham of Claverhouse, also known as 'Bonnie Dundee', took place at a point known as *Raon Ruiridh* (Rory's Field) a little to the north of the gorge. Dundee felt he could gain an advantage here as Mackay's troops, horses and waggons struggled through the narrow pass. The battle, on the evening of 27 July 1689, was short and decisive, the Jacobites routing the government army in a matter of minutes. Many fleeing men were killed in the pass as they tried to escape. Dundee himself was also killed, and without his inspirational leadership the rebellion fizzled out over the following months. Rob Roy MacGregor and his father Donald were among the Jacobite force on that day.

John Mitchell's railway viaduct

The scene today is entirely peaceful as the path continues beside the river, passing John Mitchell's fine railway viaduct and then leading up steps to the site of the Soldier's Leap, where an escapee, Donald MacBean, is said to have jumped the gorge — not a leap that many would fancy, but it is surprising what you can achieve when desperation calls and your life is threatened.

The path continues upwards to reach the Visitor Centre at the roadside. After visiting the Centre, you can either return by the same route, which is no hardship; follow the longer waymarked blue route (walk back along the road for 1 km and then pick up the signs); or take a bus back (no Sunday service).

Loch Faskally in summer

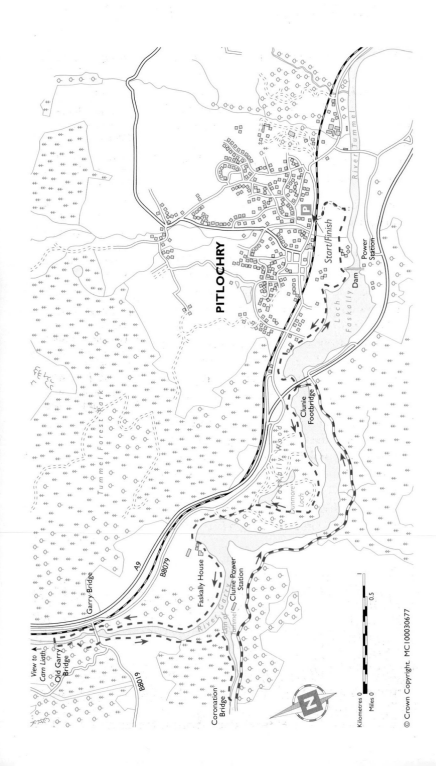

PITLOCHRY

Start/Finish

P

Power Station

Loch Faskally

Dam

Clunie Footbridge

Faskally Wood

Dunmore Loch

Tummel Forest Park

Garry Bridge

A9

B8079

Faskally House

River Garry

Linn of Tummel

Clunie Power Station

River Tummel

View to Carn Liath

Old Garry Bridge

Coronation Bridge

B8019

N

Kilometres 0   0.5
Miles 0

© Crown Copyright. MC100030677

AROUND LOCH FASKALLY

This walk, one of the longer outings in the book, makes a 'grand tour' of Loch Faskally and its surroundings and offers a variety of scene that is satisfying at any time of the year. The trees are at their best in spring, when the fresh green leaf is vivid, and in autumn, when the colours are majestic against the backdrop of loch and mountain.

From the car park, follow the road downhill and round to the right, to the car park for the Faskally Dam. Cross the access road and take the signposted footpath beside the loch. Pass a small bay and continue. At a fork keep right and at the next fork go left, still by the loch. Faskally is an artificial loch created for a hydro-electric scheme in the 1950s but is none the less attractive for that. After a further 600m go right beside a high wooden fence and then a stone wall. Turn left at the road and walk past Green Park Hotel to reach the Clunie car park (seasonal shop and café).

From here the walk follows the same outward path as Walk 1 until the Garry footbridge. Turn left as signposted and walk under the A9 bridge crossing the loch, with the Clunie footbridge beside it, somewhat dwarfed by the newer construction. Continue into Faskally Wood by a zigzag path up steps and walk through the wood, following white

INFORMATION

Distance: 16km (10 miles).

Start and finish: Ferry Road car park, Pitlochry.

Terrain: Roads, tracks and paths. No special footwear needed.

Waymarked: Partly, with blue markers.

Refreshments: Wide selection in Pitlochry. Seasonal café at Clunie car park.

Toilets: In Pitlochry.

Opening hours: Pitlochry power station and dam: mid Mar-Oct, daily 1000-1730, admission charge. Salmon ladder, exhibition on hydro-electric power, videos, shop.

Looking down on Loch Faskally

Linn of Tummel, given to the
National Trust for Scotland in 1944

marker posts. There is an attractive mixture of trees and generally a good range of birdlife to be heard, if not seen.

The path winds through the wood for about 1km and then drops down beside the pretty little Dunmore Loch, the scene brightened further in spring by a fine display of rhododendrons. Past the loch, turn left onto a road and just before reaching the Freshwater Fisheries Laboratory, turn left off the road to rejoin the lochside walk around the perimeter fence of Faskally House.

Continue, now beside the River Garry, into the Pass of Killiecrankie. The name comes from the Gaelic *coille chreithnich* meaning 'wood of aspens'. The pass is still attractively wooded with many fine broadleaved trees. Pass under the new Garry Bridge carrying the B8019 road and, a little further on, cross the river by the footbridge. Looking north up the pass there is a superb view of the gorge and, framed in its steep sides, Carn Liath ('grey hill'), one of the Beinn a' Ghlo group of hills beyond Blair Atholl.

Turn left across the bridge and walk back towards the road bridge; you are actually on an old road here. Fork left on a path signposted to Linn of Tummel. The path then passes between the river and a large hayfield. Across the field is the heavily wooded Torr an Eas ('waterfall hill'). The path climbs some steps and curves away from the Garry to reach the River Tummel, the other main feeder into Loch Faskally, at Linn of Tummel. A small plaque right down by the water here records a visit by Queen Victoria. The Linn was given to the National Trust for Scotland in 1944 by Dr Barbour of Bonskeid.

Dunmore Loch

Linn means 'pool' and Tummel is *tun allt*, 'a plunging stream', but at the time of the Queen's visit this spot was known as the Falls of Tummel. There are still attractive small waterfalls but they were higher and more impressive before the hydro-electric scheme altered the river flow. On the right here is a cutting in the rock: this was a salmon pass, built so that fish could bypass the falls. Continue by the Tummel, the path winding around in the trees, for nearly 1km to reach the pretty Coronation Bridge. Cross it and walk up to the road.

Turn left and walk along this road, which is followed for 4km above the western shore of Loch Faskally. The road carries little traffic and there are many fine views across the loch and to the south towards the Tay Valley at Ballinluig. On the way, the Clunie Power Station is passed. Beside it is a car park and picnic area which is popular with weekend visitors, and above it on the road is the Clunie Arch, built both to mark the opening of the power station and also in memory of five men who sadly lost their lives during the construction of the hydro-electric scheme.

The road curves east, looking across the loch at Faskally Wood, through which you walked earlier, and ahead to the two bridges which span the loch. One carries the busy A9; the other, which you cross, is a footbridge beside it. From the road and also from the bridge you will often see fishermen in small boats out on the loch. Once across the footbridge, turn right and retrace your outward route back to the dam. The power station and its famous fish ladder, built (like the one on the Tummel) to allow salmon to pass upriver to spawn, are open to visitors and are well worth a visit either now or later during your stay in the area.

From the dam car park continue to retrace the outward route back to the start of the walk.

Killiecrankie Gorge

The Clunie Arch

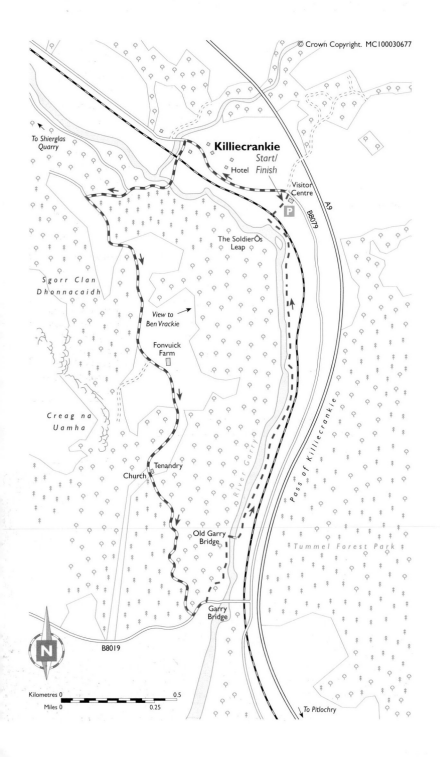

© Crown Copyright. MC100030677

To Shierglas Quarry

Killiecrankie
Start/ Finish

Hotel

Visitor Centre

P

B8079

A9

The Soldier's Leap

Sgorr Clan Dhonnacaidh

View to Ben Vrackie

Fonvuick Farm

Creag na Uamha

River Garry

Pass of Killiecrankie

Tenandry
Church

Old Garry Bridge

Tummel Forest Park

Garry Bridge

N

B8019

Kilometres 0   0.5
Miles 0   0.25

To Pitlochry

KILLIECRANKIE AND TENANDRY

This straightforward circuit is largely on quiet roads, but is no less enjoyable for that. It takes in the Pass of Killiecrankie, noted for the 1689 battle and today for its abundant wildlife and fine trees, and a lovely old church. The walk starts from the National Trust for Scotland Visitor Centre at Killiecrankie, 5km north of Pitlochry. You can visit the excellent Centre first if you wish, but I suggest doing the walk first, as this will give you a fuller appreciation of the story told in the Centre.

From the Visitor Centre, turn left (north) along the road. Keep close to the left-hand verge, as this first short section of road can be quite busy, especially in high summer. Pass the entrance to the Killiecrankie Hotel and continue down the road, noting the steep drop to the gorge on your left. The road enters Killiecrankie village, which has regular bus links with Pitlochry (no Sunday service).

Turn left (RSPB sign) and cross the railway and the River Garry. There is an interesting contrast between the upstream side, where the river is open

INFORMATION

Distance: 8km (5 miles).

Start and finish: NTS visitor centre, Killiecrankie.

Terrain: Roads and good tracks. No special footwear needed.

Refreshments and toilets: At the Visitor Centre (Apr-Oct).

Opening hours: NTS Visitor Centre, Killiecrankie: 1 Apr-31 Oct daily, 1000-1730. Admission charge for non-members. Rangers regularly lead walks—details at the Centre or from the Tourist Information Centre in Pitlochry.

Ben Vrackie from Tenandry

and broad, and downstream where it enters the gorge and flows swiftly between huge boulders. At the first junction keep left (the right fork leads to Shierglas Quarry near Blair Atholl) and at the next junction, turn left on to the Tenandry road.

The steep crag on the right, with trees somehow clinging tenaciously to it, is Sgorr Clan Dhonnacaidh. Families within this clan, which has its own museum at Calvine on the A9 north of Blair Atholl, include Reid, Robertson, MacConnachie and Duncan. The lane winds round, fringed with birch trees and with fine views of Ben Vrackie to the left.

Take the opportunity to pause and look back to the hills of the Beinn a' Ghlo group, which includes three Munros (peaks over 3000ft/914m). The principal summit rejoices in the name of *Braigh Coire Chruinn-bhalgain*, which translates as 'upland of the corrie of round blisters', a typically evocative Gaelic topographical name. The hill facing you is more simply named, as *Carn Liath* — 'grey hill' — which is certainly apt.

Just past Fonvuick Farm, a marshy area on the left by the road is enriched with lovely orchids in summer. The crag now up to the right is *Creag na*

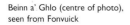
Beinn a' Ghlo (centre of photo), seen from Fonvuick

Uamha, 'crag of caves', a common name in Scotland. As you reach Tenandry, there is a superb copper beech tree beside the road, then you see the kirk, which is normally open to visitors. Its interior is fairly plain, but it has a long and interesting history. The name Tenandry comes from the Gaelic *an t-seanaontachd*, meaning 'the old agreement'.

The church dates from 1836. It was built after Mrs Christian Hay of Seggieden, owner of the Tenandry

Tenandry Kirk

estate, and her sister Miss Stewart approached the Society for the Propagation of Christian Knowledge, offering land for a church. The proposal was agreed by the General Assembly of the Church of Scotland in 1835 and the church was built with seating for 400 worshippers, the minister's stipend being set at £85 per annum.

William Grant from Nairn was chosen as the first minister, and served until 1843, preaching in both English and Gaelic. He left at the time of the Disruption, when the church establishment in Scotland was riven by disagreement over patronage – the rights of heritors (such as Mrs Hay and Miss Stewart) to nominate and approve ministers.

Peace was restored in 1850 when Pat Grant arrived, to start a ministry that was to last for 38 years. Tenandry continued to be ministered separately until 1954, when the parish was linked with Foss and Tummel. This link was severed in 1978, and since 1981 Tenandry has been what is called a 'continuing vacancy', with a number of ministers presiding over the weekly services. On 15 June 1986, the then Moderator of the General Assembly, Dr Robert Craig, preached at Tenandry to mark the kirk's 150th anniversary.

This is a lovely peaceful spot at which to pause, perhaps on the seat dedicated to the memory of Helen Victoria Barbour of Fincastle, who died in 1982 aged 91. The kirkyard contains some interesting and curious stones, including one remembering Norman Walker, Sheriff, who was born in Cumberland in 1889 and died at St Andrews in 1975. Maybe he took his holidays here and grew to love the place?

The footbridge,
Pass of Killiecrankie

From the kirk continue downhill along the lane, now in the woods again. Meet the B8109 and turn left through the car park, where an interpretation board notes that this is part of the 'Road to the Isles'. Go down steps to the left of the high bridge over the Garry. Continue on a surfaced path (this was the road before the new bridge was built) and turn right over a footbridge with fine views up the gorge. Turn left, and left again in 80m on the riverside path, noting on the right the old milestone with its legend 'Blair Atholl 3, Tummel Bridge 11'.

Continue by the river, enjoying the rush of the water and the fine trees. There is plentiful birdlife along here including finches, dippers, crows and perhaps a buzzard with its distinctive mew. You pass below the splendid railway viaduct designed by the noted engineer John Mitchell, completed in 1863 at a cost of £5,730. You could add a couple of noughts to that figure today. The viaduct is 155m (510ft) long and reaches a height of 16.5m (54ft).

The path begins to climb. At a junction go left to the Soldier's Leap, then on and up to the right to the path leading across to the Visitor Centre. Wild honeysuckle is often found in this area. The Visitor Centre has displays on the 1689 Battle of Killiecrankie and on the wildlife of the area.

Killiecrankie

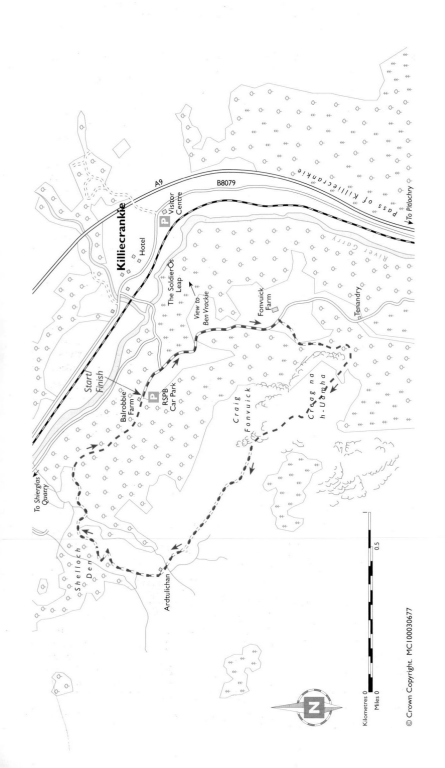

© Crown Copyright. MC100030677

KILLICRANKIE RESERVE

The Royal Society for the Protection of Birds' reserve at Killiecrankie, rising from the west bank of the River Garry, covers 530 hectares of mixed woodland, crag and open hill. From the small car park at Balrobbie Farm, two overlapping walks are laid out. A board in the car park gives seasonal information on some of the birds you may see on the walk, and a leaflet about the reserve can be obtained.

From the car park, which commands a fine view of Ben Vrackie, walk back down the access track and, at the road junction, fork right. From here to Fonvuick the route is the same as on the Tenandry circuit (Walk 3), but instead of merely admiring the crags to the right, you now have to face the prospect of climbing above them. The crags are home to jackdaws and stock doves; ravens and buzzards may also be seen.

Just before Fonvuick, turn right (yellow post) through a gate and head left of the fence to pick up a path on the right going round a grassy knoll. The path curves left around the field edge. Turn right through the next gate, then immediately left to walk along beside the dyke and fence. The path soon begins to climb as it winds round the slope, with views opening up towards Pitlochry. The path steepens, passing through an old iron gate and crossing a rushing burn. A bench here gives a welcome chance of a break.

The path turns sharp right and passes through an area rich in ferns. Among them are scaly male fern, beech fern and lemon scented fern – and of course the ubiquitous bracken, which in

INFORMATION

Distance: 7km (4 miles).

Start and finish: RSPB car park, Balrobbie Farm. Take the B8079 through Killiecrankie, turn left in the village and follow RSPB signs to the car park.

Terrain: Road and path. Some sections can be muddy. Strong footwear advised.

Waymarked: Yes, with green and yellow markers.

Refreshments: None en route. Nearest at Killiecrankie Visitor Centre or in Pitlochry.

Toilets: Killiecrankie Visitor Centre or in Pitlochry.

Public transport: Local bus from Pitlochry to Killiecrankie village. Enquire at tourist information centre for times.

Note: The RSPB ask that dogs are not taken on this walk, so that the wildlife and farm livestock are not disturbed.

Opening hours: The reserve is open dawn to dusk every day, free. Car parking charge of £1 for non-RSPB members.

A view across the glen from the reserve

Ben Vrackie from Balrobbie Farm

summer grows high on either side of the path. Among the summer birds to be seen and heard here are wood warblers and redstarts.

The path swings left below large crags and then takes a 180-degree turn right to continue up through birchwood and then larch, passing through a kissing gate. Birds hereabouts may include coal tits, chaffinches, redstarts and crossbills, and roe deer are often seen in the sheltered hollow ahead. The hollow once in fact held the house of Corhulichan, and the path crosses it on its right side to reach the ruins of the buildings. This is a good place for a stop, to pause and reflect on the way of life of the people who tended livestock, grew crops and made a living a hundred years and more ago. It is a quiet and peaceful place now.

Not long after passing the ruins, the path reaches its highest point at a lone pine. There are superb views in both directions: back to Loch Faskally and Deuchary Hill and, after a few more paces, forward to Glen Garry with Blair Castle in the centre of the picture. After this the path starts to descend. The vegetation has changed to heather moor, and you may see grouse in this area. Before long Beinn a' Ghlo is seen to the right.

After a long, steady descent, the path goes through a birch wood, which displays superb colouring in spring, when it is a vivid fresh green, and in autumn, when it glows golden against the sky. Cross a fence by a stile and continue to the edge of the wood. You can turn right here (yellow/green markers) for a shortcut back to the car park, but the full walk continues across the field, now following green markers.

Go through a gate and pass to the right of the buildings at Ardtulichan, now no longer occupied, though livestock are still kept in the fields. A feature of the reserve is that farming and conservation work together, with the grazing managed so that the farmer and the wildlife both benefit.

Cross a stile and go half left to join a grassy track. To the left is Shelloch Den, its steep sides birch-clad. You may see red squirrels here. Follow the track as it twists downhill, swinging right and then left. Cross a stile and go right again. Continue descending, cross a burn and in a further 50m, leave the track on the right and go through a kissing gate to walk beside a dyke. Go through another kissing gate and turn right for 75m, then left across the burn and up beside another dyke. On the hill here are several exclosures, areas fenced off to allow natural regeneration to take place. You can see the difference when grazing pressure is lifted.

Rejoin the yellow route, go through a metal gate, and walk along beside a fence and dyke. All this area is rich in flowers, including orchids, in summer. The path passes behind the buildings at Balrobbie to return to the car park. where as well as the reserve guide, general information on the RSPB is available. If you are not already a member, perhaps you might be tempted to join to support the very worthwhile work the Society carries out all over the country on reserves such as this.

Old Shieling, RSPB reserve

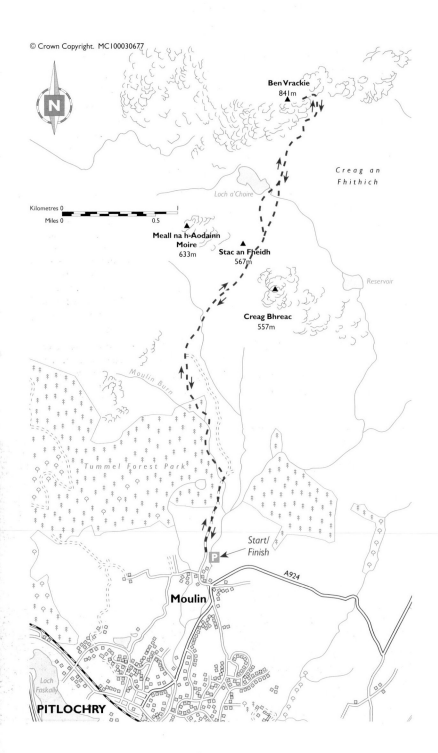

© Crown Copyright. MC100030677

BEN VRACKIE

alk out of the car park, and take the minor road opposite. At the first sharp left-hand bend, go ahead on the path which rises steadily beside the Moulin Burn through mixed woodland. This first part of the ascent is gradual. In about 500 metres, at the edge of the wood, cross the stile onto open moorland and gaze with anticipation at the scene ahead. The summit is hidden at this point but you can see the path curving away uphill and over the immediate horizon.

Follow the path, which soon provides extensive views back down the Tummel/Tay Valley. Before long you reach a memorial plaque to an Australian airman, and this is a good place to pause and take in the surroundings. The small craggy hill up on the right is Creag Bhreac. Interestingly, this name, meaning 'speckled crag', is the same as Ben Vrackie ('speckled hill'), despite the different spelling. In the latter case, *Bhreac* (pronounced Vreck) has become corrupted into Vrackie over a long period of time. There are many hills of this name in Scotland.

INFORMATION

Distance: 12km (7 miles).

Start and finish: The small car park signposted from the village of Moulin, 3km north-east of Pitlochry.

Terrain: Paths. Steep climb towards the summit. **The walk should only be undertaken in good conditions unless you are an experienced hillwalker.** Boots must be worn and good waterproofs, food and spare warm clothing carried.

Refreshments: None en route. Wide choice in Pitlochry, also the Moulin Inn.

A stunning view of Ben Vrackie

A path goes off to the left here, part of a waymarked route that climbs a little further before descending to eventually reach the Visitor Centre at Killiecrankie, but your route stays with the main summit path. It continues climbing steadily, with a fence on the right, rounding a corner below the small bluff called Stac an Fheidh ('peak of deer') to see Loch a' Choire ahead. The main path passes over a stretch of wettish ground to the right of the loch but it is easy to make a diversion to walk over to the impounding dam for this attractive little loch.

From here you can see the upper part of the hill rising more steeply ahead. The spur over to the right is Creag an Fhithich, 'crag of ravens'. If you feel at this stage that you do not wish to go to the summit, go left round the loch, meet the branch path referred to above, turn left and return down the hill.

For the summit, take a deep breath and start the hard part of the ascent. There is no need to hurry. It's not a race and you will get there in the end. Views are opening out all the time, with glimpses of the bigger hills to the north and the fine panorama back to the south always ready to catch your eye.

The path winds up, pressing relentlessly on. It goes up into a high corrie and then turns back left for the final push up to the 841m summit, with its triangulation pillar, cairn and view indicator. And what a view it is! In clear weather it seems that half of Scotland is spread out below you.

To the north-west, across Glen Girnaig, are the triple peaks of Beinn a' Ghlo, with Carn Liath, the nearest, showing by its extensive screes why it is called 'grey hill'. Further round, you look up the glen of the River Garry towards the Drumochter Pass, along the line taken by General Wade when he made his military road to Fort George at Inverness in the 1730s, the same line followed by both the A9 and the railway today.

Over to the west is the Tummel Forest Park and further away the unmistakable cone of Schiehallion. The panorama is completed by the broad strath of Tummel and Tay leading south towards Dunkeld. It is a place to linger (provided the wind is not too cold) and savour, though you are unlikely to have it to yourself, for Vrackie is a deservedly popular hill.

Queen Victoria at Balmoral

On one of her first visits to Scotland, Queen Victoria stayed at Blair Castle in 1844 and enjoyed a number of tours about the countryside here, climbing several hills. She mentions Ben Vrackie, and was clearly much impressed by the beauty of the Highland scene. These expeditions greatly influenced her decision, taken with Prince Albert, to buy the Balmoral Estate on Deeside.

The return is by the same path, and again it pays to take your time and enjoy the experience to the full. At 841 m (2760 ft), Ben Vrackie is not quite a Munro, the name given to Scottish hills over 3000ft/914m, but it is a fine hill for all that and has a summit panorama not matched by many hills of greater height.

This is not a hillwalking guide, but if your ascent of Ben Vrackie has whetted your appetite there are many excellent books and guides available describing the superlative mountains of Scotland. Or you may be perfectly content with just this one. Either way, you will have enjoyed a fine day out on a grand hill.

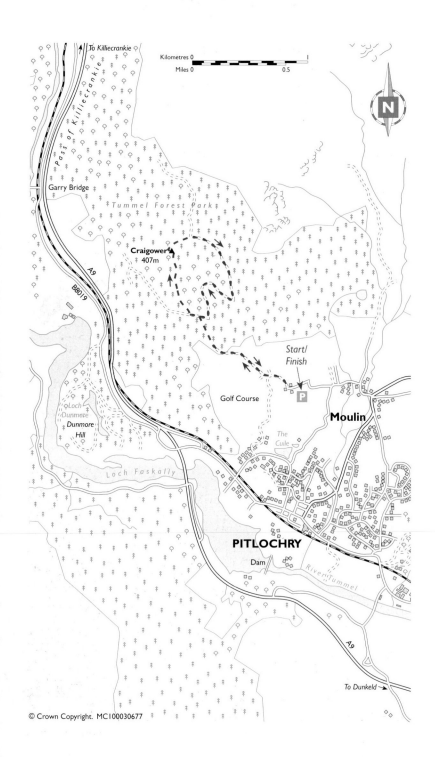

Kilometres 0   1

Miles 0   0.5

N

To Killiecrankie

Pass of Killiecrankie

Garry Bridge

Tummel Forest Park

A9

B8019

Craigower
407m

Loch
Dunmore

Dunmore
Hill

Golf Course

Start/
Finish

P

Moulin

The
Cuile

Loch Faskally

PITLOCHRY

Dam

River Tummel

A9

To Dunkeld

CRAIGOWER

The walk follows the Dunmore Trail path and leads up to a notable viewpoint. The upper part of Craigower, extending for 4.5ha, was given to the National Trust for Scotland in 1947 by the late Mrs Fergusson of Baledmund in memory of her father, Captain Wisely. The Dunmore Trail is named in memory of John, Earl of Dunmore, a member of the Trust's council and its executive committee, who died in 1980, and of his father, Viscount Fincastle, who was killed in action in 1940.

From the car park follow the road then track towards the golf course, which must surely be one of the most scenic courses anywhere in Britain. Golfers must have to concentrate hard to play their shots without being distracted by the views. Fortunately you only have to walk, look and enjoy.

Follow the track across a fairway as signposted, exercising care and crossing only when there are no golfers playing on the hole, pass the fourth tee and turn left in front of Rock Cottage. There is already a fine view back down the valley of the Tay, over Pitlochry towards Ballinluig.

INFORMATION

Distance: 7km (4 miles).

Start and finish: The small Craigower car park, reached by taking Larchwood Road out of Pitlochry signposted to the golf course and The Cuilc. Continue on Golf Course Road past the golf club car park and turn left, following the Craigower signs until a grass car park is reached next to a cottage.

Terrain: Good tracks and paths. No special footwear needed. Steep climb on to Craigower.

Waymarked: Yes, brown markers.

Refreshments: None en route. Wide choice in Pitlochry.

Pitlochry golf course

Looking west to Loch Tummel from the summit of Craigower

Follow the path inside the fence and dyke, turn right and left to enter the wood at a kissing gate with a sign for the Dunmore Trail and walk along with a stone dyke on your left, still beside the golf course. The path then turns right into the wood proper, much of which is conifer planting. Go uphill to meet a forest road, turn left for a few metres then right by a picnic table to climb steeply along a good path through tall conifers.

The path emerges from the wood with the summit of the hill rearing up ahead. Go right and steeply up a smaller path, curving round on steps to reach the summit. A viewpoint indicator shows what can be seen and explains the different types of land use in the area — agriculture, forestry and grouse moor. Conservation could perhaps be added to that list, as you are standing on a hill owned by Scotland's premier conservation body.

It is not hard to see why Craigower was a 'beacon hill' in the times when messages were passed in this way, from hilltop to hilltop. The panorama is truly outstanding. To the west, a superb long view encompasses Loch Tummel and the distant peaks around Rannoch Moor, with Glencoe visible in clear conditions. To the left is the unmistakable cone of Schiehallion. Turning right, the view extends up the Pass of Killiecrankie to Blair Atholl and beyond, with the massif of Beinn a' Ghlo at far right. The valley with its traffic seems far below.

Before starting back down, take the path on the left to a seat with another lovely view, this time over Pitlochry and Loch Faskally. On the way you pass a 'hibernaculum' set up by the National Trust for Scotland to provide a winter refuge for lizards, slow-worms and adders. It consists of a number of chambers below ground which provide a safe place for reptiles to hibernate.

Walk back to the view indicator and start the return as waymarked, down a path to the right. Ben Vrackie can soon be seen ahead. The path winds through a rather dense plantation to reach the forest road. Turn right past a large Cellnet aerial and follow the road as it twists steadily downhill round several bends. Just when you are wondering which way you are facing, a final right-hand bend brings you back to the outward route.

Follow the waymarkers

Watch carefully for the marker, which is facing away from you. Turn left and walk down past the golf course, across the fairway and back to the car park.

Another fine view of Pitlochry golf course

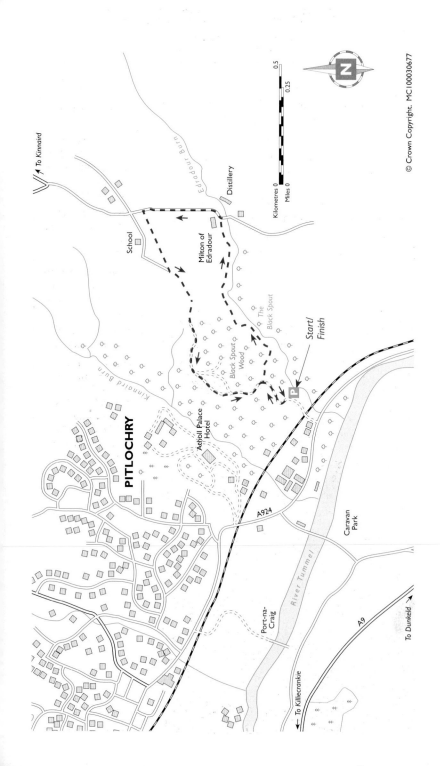

To Kinnaird

Edradour Burn

Distillery

School

Milton of
Edradour

The Black Spout

Black Spout Wood

Start/
Finish

Kinnaird Burn

PITLOCHRY

Atholl Palace
Hotel

A924

Port-na-
Craig

River Tummel

Caravan
Park

A9

To Killiecrankie

To Dunkeld

Kilometres 0
Miles 0

0.25

0.5

© Crown Copyright. MCl00030677

THE BLACK SPOUT AND EDRADOUR

This varied walk takes in a fine waterfall and an intriguing distillery which is open to visitors. From the car park, turn right following the Black Spout sign, and at the fork keep right. The imposing turrets of the Atholl Palace Hotel appear over the trees to the left.

At the next junction turn right following a signpost to the Black Spout and Edradour, and climb steadily through a beautiful mature birchwood. At another fork, go right to reach the viewing platform for the Black Spout. The platform has been provided by the Rotary Club of Pitlochry and was built by Aberdeen University OTC in July 1989.

The Black Spout Falls

INFORMATION

Distance: 5km (3 miles).

Start and finish: Black Spout Wood car park, signposted off the main road at the south end of Pitlochry.

Terrain: Paths and tracks. Strong footwear needed in wet conditions.

Refreshments: Wide selection in Pitlochry, plus your free dram at Edradour!

Toilets: In Pitlochry and at the distillery.

Opening hours: Edradour Distillery: Mar-Oct, Mon-Sat 0930-1700, Sun 1200-1700. Nov-mid Dec, Mon-Sat 1000-1600. Jan and Feb, shop only, no tours.

It provides a spectacular view of the triple fall, which is seen at its best after a period of rain. A short top fall drops to a dark pool, then the longer central fall thunders down to another pool. Finally a waterslide over rocks brings the cataract to the burn at the foot of the gorge. The total drop is around 60m and it makes a splendid sight — and sound.

From the falls, go uphill through the woods (signposted Edradour), passing the lip of the falls. The path winds around as if unsure which direction to take. When the path forks go right, and at the field corner carry on along the narrow path between the field fence and the dyke. There is a superb view of Ben Vrackie to the left. Re-enter the wood and follow the path up to the road.

Over to the right is Colivoulin Farm. The name means 'mill wood', indicating that the rushing burn once powered a mill here, and indeed the settlement is still named as Milton of Edradour on some maps. At the road, turn right for a few metres to reach the entrance to the distinctive buildings of Edradour Distillery.

Founded in 1825, Edradour prides itself on being the smallest distillery in Scotland and the last to produce a handcrafted malt whisky in limited quantity. The essential ingredients for whisky are water and grain. Edradour's water comes from

Edradour, the smallest distillery in Scotland

high on Moulin Moor, based on granite, and passes through peat to give it a special character. The distillery uses local barley, malted and dried over peat fires.

There are regular tours so that visitors can see the distilling process, starting with the mash tun, where water and barley are soaked together to make 'wort', which then ferments with brewer's yeast. The mixture, now called 'wash', goes to the stills. The copper stills at Edradour are the smallest size permitted under Excise rules. The stillman's skill in selecting the spirit is a vital part of the whole process.

The end product is a clear spirit, 70 degrees proof. It is matured in sherry casks, especially imported from Spain, for at least ten years before being bottled. At the end of your tour you can taste the result and appreciate why the Gaelic name for whisky is *uisgebaugh*, 'the water of life'. Edradour has an excellent shop where souvenirs can be bought.

Fortified by your dram, continue the walk by turning right out of the distillery on the road. This was once part of the old North Road, which passed through Moulin rather than Pitlochry. There is a lovely view across Strathtummel to the west. In 200m, leave the road on the left to take a narrow fenced path which turns left, parallel to a driveway.

At the field corner, turn left on a track, walking downhill with views of Pitlochry ahead. At farm buildings, re-enter the wood through an iron kissing gate. Continue downhill (signposted to Pitlochry). At the next junction, keep left on the main track, ignoring the sign to Pitlochry. Stay on this track, which continues downhill through the wood and eventually returns you to the car park.

The wood includes many fine mature trees. In spring, parts of the floor are carpeted with the white-flowered wood anemone. If you are lucky, you may see a roe deer in the trees, or perhaps spot a red squirrel scampering back to its nest, called a drey. The birdlife includes woodpeckers, which can sometimes be heard hammering away at dead trees for food.

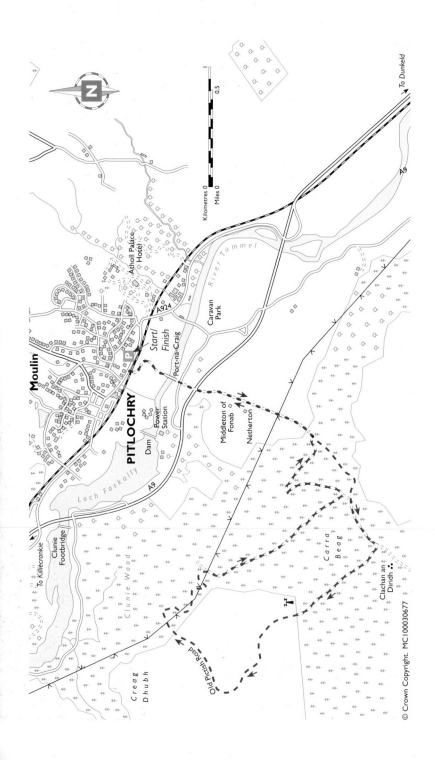

MOORS AND MEGALITHS

This very varied walk is deservedly popular with both locals and visitors. From the car park, walk down the road (signposted for the Festival Theatre and Port-na-Craig) and once round the right-hand bend, take the path on the left signed to the Festival Theatre.

Cross the River Tummel by a fine suspension bridge which has a distinct 'bounce' to it as you walk across. Upstream is the dam impounding Loch Faskally, and across the river is the settlement of Port-na-Craig. You will see that the first house is called Ferryman's Cottage. There were ferries across most of Scotland's rivers in the times before bridges were frequent, and the names of many such places have survived.

Down by the far bank is a brick pillar with a water level marker. This is a gauging station operated by the Tay River Purification Board. It records the water flow every half hour and is linked to a central computer in the Board's

INFORMATION

Distance: 11km (7 miles).

Start and Finish: Ferry Road car park, Pitlochry (pay and display).

Terrain: Good tracks and paths. Special footwear only needed in wet conditions.

Waymarked: Yes, brown markers, as Clunie Walk.

Refreshments: Wide choice in Pitlochry.

Toilets: In Pitlochry.

Note: When timber operations are being carried out, parts of this route may be closed. If so please follow diversion signs.

Dramatic moorland scenery

headquarters in Perth. These gauging stations become vitally important during times of flood, such as happened in January 1993 following a week of heavy snowfall, rapid thaw and torrential rain.

At 5.15am on Saturday 16 January, a flow of 1047 cubic metres per second (cumecs) was recorded here, the highest ever at this station (an average daily maximum would be between 150 and 200 cumecs), and at that time the water was 5.1m above gauge zero. Add that to all the water rushing down the Tay and it is little wonder that much of the farmland in this area was inundated and Perth itself was severely affected.

These things rarely affect the visitor but they are a reminder of the awesome power of nature. Continue over the bridge and on reaching the road turn left, cross a minor road and continue uphill on a road. Now comes the most dangerous part of the walk—crossing the very busy A9. Take your time and cross **with great care**, continuing up the lane opposite to pass through the well-kept Middleton of Fonab farm and on uphill along a track between fences. Past Netherton, pause at the gate for a splendid view back over Pitlochry.

Ben Vrackie looms over Pitlochry

Clachan an Diridh

The track continues climbing steadily to enter woodland and zigzags up through the trees. Turn left onto a path as signposted (this is also the right of way to Strathtay), go through a gate at the entry to Fonab Forest and continue, still climbing, with pines to the right and a birchwood to the left. The lovely old grassy path winds up, and before long you see a heather moor to the left. The hill is called Carra Beag ('little rock').

The gradient eases and the path joins a forest road which is followed for about a kilometre, over generally level ground. At a junction of tracks the walk turns right, but it is worth continuing for about 200m and taking a small path on the right to see Clachan an Diridh, a small group of much-weathered standing stones. The name may mean 'the upright stones' but little is known of their history. I always feel a tremendous sense of atmosphere at such places, knowing that the megaliths have stood here for thousands of years.

Above: Enjoying the walk across
the moor
Top: The Old Pictish Road across
heather moorland

Return to the junction of tracks and turn left.
Follow the track to the forest edge and go through
a gate onto the open moor, with aerial masts up
to your right at the summit of An Suidhe ('the
seat'). Follow the path as it winds across the

heather moor, glorious with rich purple in autumn. There are wonderful views all around. Ahead is Ben Vrackie, with the Beinn a' Ghlo group to its left, while to the west the hills above Aberfeldy are crowned by Farragon Hill.

The path, which is steadily being improved, climbs steadily to give another fine view to the west before starting to descend and swinging right. You may well see, or at least hear, grouse on this section, their 'go back, go back' call unmistakable. The next section of the path is said to be on the route of an old Pictish Road. If it is, its makers had a fine eye for a scenic route and with its sense of space, this is a place to savour at all times of the year.

Re-enter the forest at a gate and follow the path round to the right to reach, and briefly follow, a broad path under electricity pylons. The path climbs steeply, and swings this way and that in a contorted manner, crossing the forest ride twice before finally taking a straighter line through the trees. At the highest point, next to a pylon, there is a broad view down the Tay Valley.

At a fork, go right, slightly uphill. You soon join a forest road, still climbing but at a comfortable gradient before the road starts to descend. At a junction, go very sharply left, downhill, and in 500 metres go equally sharply right. There are big mature pines to the left and their scent is marked here.

In about 500m go through a gate and shortly afterwards rejoin the outward route, passing down through the farm, recrossing the A9 (again taking great care) and so back down to Pitlochry. Please keep a sharp eye open for the right turn to the suspension bridge — it is easily missed. Alternatively, you could continue to the dam or the theatre if you wanted a different end to the walk.

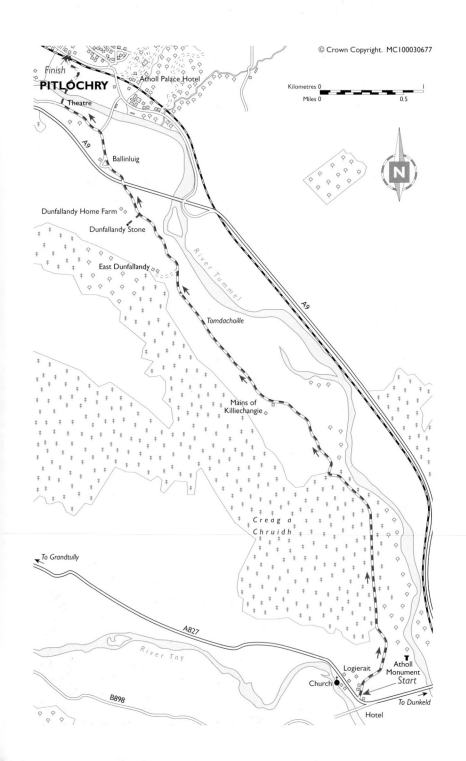

© Crown Copyright. MC100030677

Finish
PITLOCHRY
Atholl Palace Hotel
Theatre
A9
Ballinluig
Dunfallandy Home Farm
Dunfallandy Stone
East Dunfallandy
River Tummel
Tomdachoille
A9
Mains of
Killiechangie
Creag a
Chruidh
To Grandtully
A827
River Tay
B898
Logierait
Church
Atholl
Monument
Start
To Dunkeld
Hotel

Kilometres 0   1
Miles 0   0.5

N

ROB ROY AND THE PICTS

INFORMATION

Distance: 7km (4 miles).

Start: Logierait village, reached by bus from Pitlochry—enquire at the tourist information centre for times.

Finish: Pitlochry.

Terrain: All on roads. No special footwear needed.

Refreshments: Logierait Inn, wide choice in Pitlochry.

Although this walk is all on roads, it has plenty of interest and there is generally little traffic to trouble the walker. Start by visiting Logierait's neat church. There has been a church or chapel on this site since the 7th century. The present building dates from 1805 and was renovated in 1928 and again in 1971, internally. A stone on the church wall commemorates Alexander Mackenzie, born here in 1822, who became Prime Minister of Canada in 1875. Another, more recent son of the parish who has achieved fame is Dennis Mann, whose engraved glass trophies were given to the winner of the popular BBC television quiz *Mastermind* each year.

There is a Pictish cross in the kirkyard dating back to the 10th century and also three 'mortsafes', iron cages used to protect graves from bodysnatchers in the early 19th century when unscrupulous people sold corpses to medical schools. There are also a number of memorial stones to members of the Butter family, notable locally for many generations.

The name Logierait seems to be accepted by linguistic scholars as a corruption of *Lagan m-Choid*, 'the hollow of St Coed', who founded the first church here. Logierait is notable today for having a lady minister, the Rev. Christine Creegan.

Leave the church and walk back through the village, noting, behind the Logierait Hotel, the bridge across the Tay which carried the former railway line from Aberfeldy. The branch from Ballinluig was opened in July 1865, with a station at Grandtully,

Logierait's historic kirk

The Atholl Monument

and lasted exactly 100 years before falling victim to the Beeching cuts in May 1965. Some parts of the old line are walkable but much has now been lost.

Turn left up the minor road signposted to Dunfallandy and Hillhead. It climbs steeply for a short while before levelling out past a small, neat cemetery, and then becomes a narrow lane with little traffic, signed as a cycleway. To the right, peeping out of the trees, you may see a stone cross. This is the top of a large and impressive monument to the 6th Duke of Atholl, erected on this site in 1866 'by the inhabitants of Athole and numerous friends in testimony of their regard and esteem for his character'. A path leads up to the monument from the riverbank but it is not accessible from this side.

Also in this area was Logierait's old castle, which has associations with Rob Roy MacGregor, who you will find, if you read his true story, was not at all the fearsome brigand and outlaw he has been made out to be. He was a man of his time, and that was a time of much rivalry between factions in Scotland. Rob had enemies, as did many others like him.

In 1717 Rob had fallen out with the then Duke of Atholl, who managed to capture him at Dunkeld through a subterfuge and brought him to Logierait under heavy escort on 3 June of that year. Within three days Rob was free. One of his clansmen brought a message, supposedly from Rob's wife, and the guards, whom Rob had taken care to flatter and amuse, were less vigilant than they should have been. They let Rob out of the door to read the message and in a flash he was on his clansman's horse and away. The Duke, who had already boasted of capturing Rob, was naturally mortified. 'Roy' in his name comes from the Gaelic *ruadh* meaning red — as it does in the placenames Glen Roy and Roy Bridge near Fort William.

Continue along the road, with a beautiful view of Ben Vrackie framed in trees. There is forestry to the left and high above pylons you can see Creag a' Chruidh (possibly 'crag of the Picts', from the Gaelic *Cruithnigh* for that race). The road winds round several bends before reaching Woodend Cottage, after which it dips and then climbs quite steeply past Mains of Killiechangie, which has a quite splendid prospect over Strath Tummel to Pitlochry, with the Atholl Palace Hotel prominent, and Ben Vrackie rising behind the town. The placename seems to be derived from 'the cell of Coemhi', an obscure Celtic saint.

After this the road passes through attractive birchwood. The trend is now definitely downhill but there is one more short climb before Tomdachoille ('wooded hill') is passed. There are plenty of blackberry bushes along here — good for an autumn walk!

Past East Dunfallandy with its collection of caravans the road emerges into the open again with the A9 bridge over the Tummel to the right and again a fine view over Pitlochry to the hills. At the entry to Dunfallandy Home Farm, go left and follow the signs to view the Dunfallandy Stone in its protective glass case. The stone is thought to date from the 9th century. The front is a cross of ornamental panels flanked by angels and beasts. On the back, framed by two serpents, are seated figures and enigmatic Pictish symbols. Much research has been done on these stones in recent years but in truth they remain as mysterious as the people who carved them.

The mysterious Dunfallandy stone, dating from the 9th century

Return to the road and turn left to pass under the A9. Go through the hamlet of Ballinluig, noting that the name is the same as that of the village a few kilometres south. This is not uncommon in Scotland. At the junction, turn left, and at the next junction, with the Festival Theatre ahead, go right and right again over the suspension bridge, after which it is a short walk into the centre of Pitlochry.

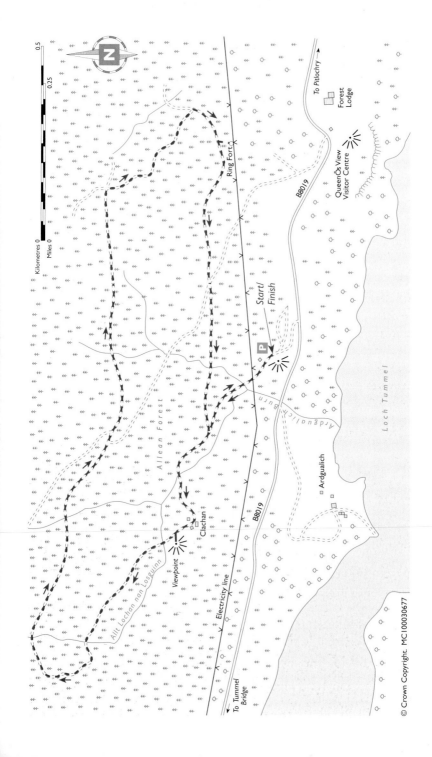

Kilometres 0
Miles 0
0.25
0.5

N

To Pitlochry

Forest
Lodge

Queen's View
Visitor Centre

B8019

Ring Fort

Start/
Finish

P

Ardgualich Burn

Allean Forest

Loch Tummel

Ardgualich

Electricity line

B8019

Clachan

Viewpoint

Allt Lochan nan Losguinn

To Tummel
Bridge

ALLEAN FOREST

This short, straightforward but nonetheless interesting walk is one of a number laid out in the Tay Forest Park by Forest Enterprise. From the car park, follow the main forest track uphill. The walk, known as the Ring Fort Walk, follows red waymarkers all the way. You may also see red and white numbered posts. These are not for a walk, but are part of a Wayfinding course. Wayfinding is the non-competitive introductory form of the navigational sport of orienteering; further details can be obtained at the Queen's View Visitor Centre if you are interested.

The track continues climbing through mature conifers, with a large cleared area on the right, to reach the old Clachan. This small settlement of three houses (one re-roofed in turf), small fields used for cultivation and a kiln for drying corn was probably established in the early 18th century and abandoned perhaps a hundred years later. It has a fine location on a south-facing slope and the inhabitants would have been largely self-sufficient, keeping a few sheep and cattle and

INFORMATION

Distance: 5km
(3 miles).

Start and finish:
Signposted car park
800m west of the
Queen's View Visitor
Centre on B8019.

Terrain: Good forest
tracks and paths. No
special footwear
needed.

Waymarked: Yes, red
markers.

Refreshments:
None en route.
Tearoom at Queen's
View.

Toilets: At start of
walk and at Queen's
View.

The old Clachan

Charlie Easterfield's sleeping wood sculpture

growing their own crops and vegetables. After the breakdown of the clan system and the rise of large estates practising sheep-farming, such places became impossible to sustain.

A path on the left leads in 200m to a viewpoint. Take away the forest and this would be the view enjoyed by the people of the Clachan, encompassing Loch Tummel and the hills around, topped by Schiehallion, the 'fairy hill of the Caledonians', which rises to 1083m and is now partly owned by the John Muir Trust. The loch was lower until the 1950s, when its level was raised as part of a hydro-electric scheme. At the viewpoint is a wood sculpture by Charlie Easterfield showing a sleeping figure.

Return to the track, turn left and continue uphill. The trees become more mixed, with birch in among the pines. Birds to be seen and heard in the forest include jay, siskin, crossbill, goldcrest and lesser redpoll; mammals include squirrels, foxes and both red and roe deer. The track makes a big loop to the right, crossing the Allt Lochan nan Losguinn twice (it is a small burn and not a major feature), and then opening out to give a wider view ahead. The track starts to descend gently, and after about 500m the yellow route goes off to the right. The cleared area to the right here has opened the view greatly.

Keep on the track, climbing a little. Through the trees on the right there are glimpses of Farragon Hill, Beinn Eagagach and back to Schiehallion. Beinn Eagagach is the site of mines where barytes, a mineral widely used in lubrication, is extracted.

Reach a T-junction and turn right, leaving the track for a surfaced path that winds downhill to meet another track. Turn right here. The loch is soon glimpsed through the trees, and after 200 metres, turn left as signposted to view the ring fort. This ancient stronghold, thought to date from the 8th century, commands a tremendous view westward, unfortunately rather spoiled by an overhead power line going right through the site. The fort, which may have been roofed, is about 10m in diameter with thick walls, and the strengthened west gateway can still be seen clearly.

Return to the track and turn left. It is all downhill now. The yellow route comes down from the right at Wayfinding marker S9, and the main track is then soon visible ahead. Turn left and walk back down to the car park.

The Queen's View Visitor Centre is well worth a visit. It has an excellent exhibition on forestry planning and development, an audio-visual programme, a shop with interesting souvenirs and books, a tearoom and toilets. Also here is the Queen's View itself, admired by Queen Victoria in 1866 but already named before that time, in honour, it is thought, of Isabella, queen of Robert the Bruce.

Queen's View, named in honour of Isabella, queen of Robert the Bruce

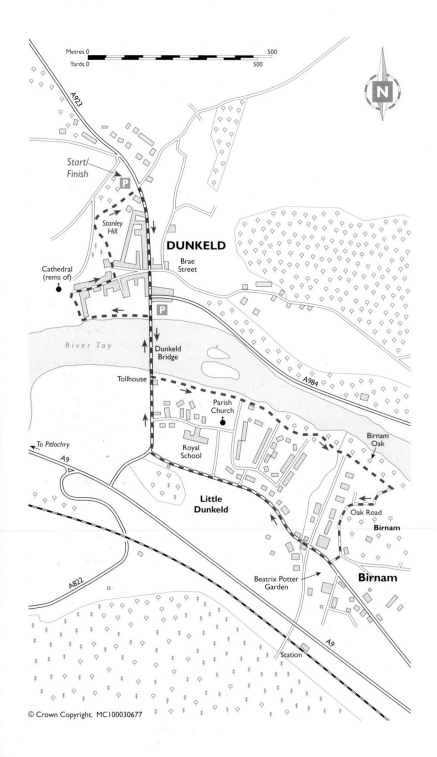

Metres 0 — 500
Yards 0 — 500

A923

Start/ Finish

P

Stanley Hill

DUNKELD

Cathedral (rems of)

Brae Street

P

River Tay

Dunkeld Bridge

Tollhouse

A984

Parish Church

To Pitlochry

A9

Royal School

Birnam Oak

Little Dunkeld

Oak Road

Birnam

A822

Beatrix Potter Garden

Birnam

A9

Station

N

© Crown Copyright. MC100030677

HISTORIC DUNKELD AND BIRNAM

There are many walks with literary associations, but there can be few which link, in a short step, two such startlingly different figures. Within a couple of minutes you pass from the medieval drama of Shakespeare's *Macbeth* to the enchanted world of Mrs Tiggywinkle, Jeremy Fisher and Peter Rabbit.

Leave the car park to turn right towards the bridge over the Tay. The main street is full of interesting shops, cafes and an art gallery. Dunkeld was largely destroyed in a battle in 1689, but many of the buildings erected shortly after that time have been carefully preserved.

Continue to Telford's superb bridge over the River Tay. Walk over the bridge and at the far side, by the attractive old tollhouse, turn left down steps to the riverside. Turn right and walk along the riverside path (signposted to the Birnam Oak).

There are many fine trees along this stretch, and usually plenty of birdlife on the river. Pass behind the parish church and cross the Inchewan Burn by a footbridge. Over the bridge go half-right then ahead on the main path to reach the Birnam Oak, said to be the last survivor of the wood made famous by the witches' prophecy in *Macbeth*: 'fear not, till Birnam Wood do come to Dunsinane'.

INFORMATION

Distance: About 5.5km (3.5 miles).

Terrain: Pavements and good paths. No special footwear needed.

Start and finish: North car park, Dunkeld (pay and display).

Toilets: At the start, in Birnam, and in the square beside the tourist information centre.

Refreshments: Excellent selection of cafés and hotels in both Dunkeld and Birnam.

Opening Hours: Dunkeld Cathedral: Apr-Sept: Mon-Sat 0930-1900, Sun 1400-1900; Oct-Mar: Mon-Sat 0930-1600, Sun 1400-1600.
Ell Shop: Jun-Aug: Mon-Sat 1000-1700, Sun 1400-1700; Apr-May and Sep-Dec: Mon-Sat 1000-1300, 1400-1700.
Scottish Horse Regimental Museum: Easter and Jun-Sept daily 1000-1200, 1400-1700.
Beatrix Potter Exhibition, Birnam Institute: daily 1000-1700.
Tourist Information Centre: All year, daily 0930-1730 (tel: 01350 727688).

Dunkeld Cathedral

The story is that in 1054 soldiers cut branches and foliage here to use as camouflage on their way to a battle at Dunsinane Hill, 20km to the south-east.

The Beatrix Potter Garden

Continue past the Oak for a short way to a flight of steps on the right. Climb the steps and pass to the right of Jubilee Park and play area. Turn right at its end and left into Oak Road to reach the centre of Birnam. The name, Norse in origin, means 'village of the warrior'. On the right is the imposing Birnam Hotel. A typically grandiose Victorian building, it was opened in the 1850s, at the time that the railway reached Birnam. The row of houses on the left, Murthly Terrace, was built in the 1860s as summer lodges for holiday visitors coming by train.

Cross the road into the Beatrix Potter Garden, opened in 1992. There are imaginative sculptures of several of the famous characters from the children's stories. Beatrix spent many happy holidays in this area as a girl and young woman, and some of her best-loved characters are based on people she met at that time. After enjoying the garden, it is worth visiting the excellent exhibition on Beatrix's life and work in the Birnam Institute next to it (café and toilets). As well as writing the famous stories, she was also a notable student of fungi and in later life, in the Lake District, became renowned as a breeder of Herdwick sheep.

To continue the walk, re-cross the road and turn left past imposing iron gates, crowned with four gilt lions. Walk past the driveway to the church and the Royal School of Dunkeld, founded in 1567. Go half right across a green and re-cross the bridge over the Tay.

Once over the bridge, turn sharply right and go

down and under the bridge, then along the riverbank. From here you can see the full splendour of Telford's five-arched bridge, which after nearly 200 years looks as strong as ever. Continue on grass as far as the cathedral wall. Turn right and walk up to the gates to enter the cathedral grounds. The cathedral was begun in 1318; the nave and north-west tower date from the 15th century. Sacked during the Reformation, the church was re-roofed in the 1660s, and still serves as the parish church for Dunkeld today. Its grounds contain many fine trees.

After visiting the cathedral, walk down Cathedral Street. You are now on the Dunkeld Heritage Trail. No. 9 was the childhood home of Alexander Mackenzie, later Prime Minister of Canada. On the corner of the main square is the Ell House, named for the ell measure — used in textiles — which is still affixed to its wall. Part of the building is now a shop, run by the National Trust for Scotland.

Jeremy Fisher

The Trust, in association with local authorities, has restored many houses in Dunkeld to a very high standard. In the square is the Scottish Horse Regimental Museum, the tourist information centre, and public toilets; on their left is the Duchess Anne, a building established in 1851 as a girls' school by Anne, Duchess of Atholl. It is now the church hall. In the centre of the square is the ornate Atholl Memorial Fountain, built in 1866 to honour the memory of the 6th Duke of Atholl, who had introduced a piped water supply to Dunkeld.

Pass through the gateway beside the toilets and walk around Stanley Hill, a tree-covered mound and open space given to the people of Dunkeld in 1958 by Cairngorm Investments. This may possibly be the *dun* or fort from which Dunkeld ('fort of the Caledonians') gets its name. At the far side of the hill you reach the car park and the end of the walk.

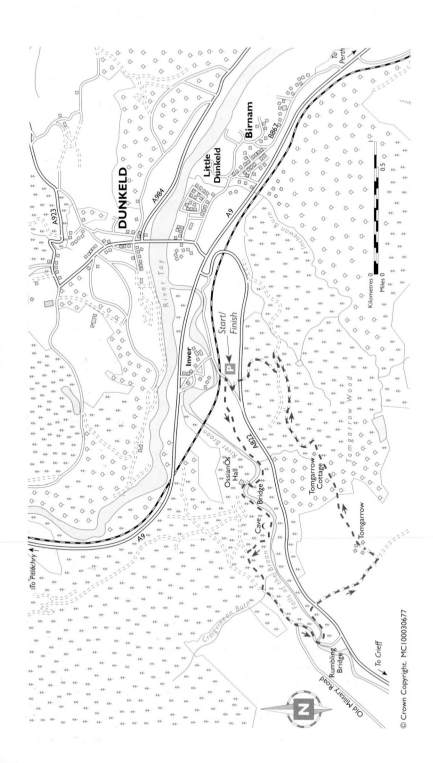

THE BRAAN AND RUMBLING BRIDGE

This very varied walk includes fine water-falls, a historic track and excellent views. From the car park, take the signposted Braan walk along a track through fine old woodland with some splendidly massive trees. The track is well used by mountain bikers, so be prepared to move aside to let them pass. Beside the path is a striking carved wooden sculpture like a double helix.

On reaching the lovely old 18th-century bridge over the Braan, note the superb Cedar of Lebanon towering over it, cross the bridge and then go up to look at the folly called Ossian's Hall. It was built in 1758 by the nephew of the 2nd Duke of Atholl (himself later the 3rd Duke) as a surprise for his uncle. The interior was decorated in 1783. At that time, visitors entered to see a painting of the bard Ossian singing to a group of maidens.

The waterfall could be heard but not seen until the guide operated a device which withdrew the painting into the wall, giving entry to a second room which was covered with mirrors, giving the extraordinary illusion of water pouring in every direction. The Hall was seriously damaged in 1869, but after being presented to the National Trust for Scotland, along with the surrounding woodland, in 1944 by Katharine, Duchess of Atholl, it was restored.

After viewing the folly — and the fine spectacle of the falls crashing down over the rocks below — continue westward along the riverside path, passing a seat dedicated to the memory of Frank McGowan, Archdeacon of Sarum (otherwise called Salisbury — a

INFORMATION

Distance: 8km (5 miles).

Start and finish: Car park at Inver, reached by turning off the A9 on to the A822 Crieff road, then turning immediately right (signposted to Inver). After 400m take the left fork, cross the railway, and the car park is 100m ahead on the right.

Terrain: Paths, tracks and roads. Strong footwear recommended.

Waymarked: Yes, green markers.

Refreshments: None en route. Nearest in Dunkeld or Birnam.

Opening hours: The Hermitage: Open all year, free.

Archway at The Hermitage

long way from here). A plantation of Norway spruce gives way to more open Scots pine. You may well see red squirrels in this area.

Continue past more falls to Ossian's Cave, a stone beehive hut with two entrances. Like the Hall, it has no real connection with Ossian but

The Hermitage viewpoint

makes the basis of a nice story nonetheless. It was constructed around the time (1762) that James Macpherson published his claimed translation of the poems of Ossian, the Celtic bard who sang of the great deeds of his warrior father Fingal. Macpherson's works were later shown to be fakes, but there was a great enthusiasm for the Ossian story and many grottoes and follies were erected in his name.

Carry on along the main path, which after a further 200m begins to curve right, away from the river. The crowds have now been left behind and for the rest of the walk there will be fewer people about. Cross over a track and continue, climbing slightly before re-entering woods.

The spectacular Falls of Braan at Rumbling Bridge

The path swings right, then turns left to cross the Craigvinean Burn by a wooden footbridge (signposted to Rumbling Bridge). Continue on a wide grassy path across pasture. This is marked on maps as 'Old Military Road', a term commonly associated with General George Wade, who initiated the great road-building programme in the Highlands after the 1715 Rising. This path you are on is part of the route between Coupar Angus and Amulree, linking with the main routes up to Fort George (near Inverness) in the east and Fort William in the west. As with many of these roads, it was Wade's successor, Major Caulfeild, who oversaw the building, in the 1740s.

The path continues to meet a lane. The original line of the Military Road carried straight on towards Ballinloan (where the tenants blocked the road in 1751 while waiting for a new bridge), but this walk goes left, down to Rumbling Bridge, for the building of which the Commissioners of Roads granted the princely sum of £10 in 1774.

It was a job well done and the bridge is still sturdy today. On its right, the Braan crashes and thunders down big rock steps into its gorge, which is a long way below you to the left of the bridge.

Cross the bridge: there is access on the right to the rocks above the lip of the falls, and this is a *very* impressive place to stand. Please take great care.

Return to the road and after a further 70m take a small path into the woods on the left. It climbs and dips, then crosses two burns by footbridges, before swerving right to the A822 road. On the way there are two viewpoints, looking first up and then downriver. Cross the A822 with care and carry on along the track ahead (signposted as a public footpath to Glen Garr).

Follow the track as it climbs steadily. To the right (south) a fine view of distant Glendevon opens up. After about 400m a fence comes in from the left and continues as a stone dyke. In a further 200m, just before a cattle grid, turn left through a gate onto another track.

Past the abandoned farmhouse of Tomgarrow a splendid view northwards along the Tay Valley opens up. Continue with the track and cross a stile to enter Tomgarrow Wood, which mainly consists of old birches. Pass Tomgarrow Cottage, then continue for about 150m before turning right over a small burn and through a gate in a high deer fence into conifer forest.

In 100m turn left along a main track, and at a junction shortly after that continue straight over.

Dunkeld Cathedral in Spring

Carry on along a good track with a spruce plantation to the right and more fine northward views to the left. The gap made by the Tay through Dunkeld is very clear. In 700m, at a major junction, go very sharply back left (a 180 degree turn). At the next junction in 200m, continue right with the main track.

Keep with the track (also used by mountain bikes) as it swings round left, downhill, then goes right through a gate to the A822. Cross *with great care* and follow the track ahead as it wriggles down to the minor road. The car park is a few paces to the right.

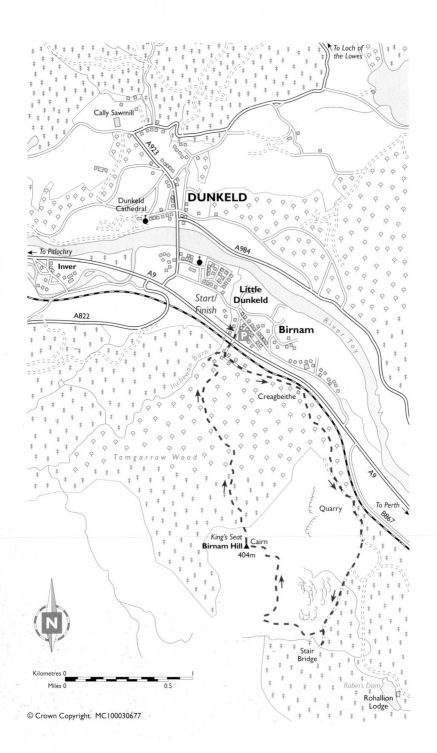

BIRNAM HILL

Starting and finishing this walk at the railway station, as well as being logical, offers the opportunity for people based elsewhere to make this a convenient outing between trains. The walk goes to the top of a hill which is noted as a fine viewpoint, and also has associations with Macbeth.

From the station car park, head north and go down the steps to the path. Turn left and cross under the railway, taking the path which climbs to the left of the road. The path emerges onto a road; go left along the road following the Birnam Hill signpost. You pass a number of fine detached houses.

Past the last house, Craigmore, on the left, the road becomes a track. At a turning circle there is a waymarker pointing ahead. Walk through fine mature trees including a number of lovely old birches. The track is on a kind of shelf with the hill sloping down to your left and up — the way you are heading before long — to your right.

At a right-hand bend, take a path going off to the left to pass well below the house called Creagbeithe ('birch crag'), and drop down markedly to a point quite close to the railway before starting to climb again, passing through open woodland. The path divides briefly, then the two paths rejoin before

INFORMATION

Distance: 8km (5 miles).

Start and finish: Dunkeld and Birnam railway station, just off the A9. If arriving by car please park in Birnam village and walk up to the station.

Terrain: Minor road, tracks and paths. Some can be muddy in wet periods. Steep ascent and descent. Strong footwear essential.

Waymarked: Yes, red markers.

Refreshments: None on route. Good selection in Birnam. The Birnam Institute (see below) is recommended.

Opening Hours: The Birnam Institute is open 1000-1700 daily. Excellent exhibition on the life of Beatrix Potter, shop, and a very good café.

The view towards the River Tay from Birnam Hill

Rock and heather near the summit of Birnam Hill

The path to the summit

reaching a junction at an open grassy area. Go right over a small burn at the point where a seat offers a pleasant view.

The path soon begins to climb in earnest, and then drops down just as sharply towards the quarry car park. The long-disused quarry, up to the right, has very impressive sheer faces now somewhat masked by trees. Continue along a broad track. Ignore the first path on the right and in about 300m turn sharp right uphill along a clear signposted path throught the trees. The path continues climbing, and eventually, after a long, steady climb, meets a track beside a stone dyke. Keep going uphill, on a slightly easier gradient.

After about 250m you pass a small grotto on the right with an attractive little waterfall running through it. Continue with the track, now level and grassy, until the junction for Stair Bridge, a clear fork, is reached. A diversion of only about 200m to the left leads you down to the lovely old Stair Bridge, which commands a very fine view to Rohallion Lodge, the lake called Robin's Dam in front of the house and Rohallion Loch beyond. The Birnham Burn gurgles through a miniature gorge below. This is a curious name, both for the aberrant 'h' and also as the burn does not flow down to Birnam!

Return to the main track and turn left, now climbing steadily again. In about 500m it reaches a fence corner and swings right, with the summit of the hill now seen ahead and the views opening up. Curlew, buzzard and skylark are often heard here between spring and autumn. Wind round with the track, which becomes a path and then turns off to the left to thread its way up through rocks to the summit. A pause before the final ascent enables the still expanding view to be enjoyed again.

The last part of the climb is very steep, with steps to help you. The slope eases and the path jinks first right and left before arriving at a large cairn on the 404m summit, named King's Seat. There is indeed a royal panorama over the Tay Valley in both directions and east to Loch of the Lowes and beyond. To the north is the distinctive high cone of Schiehallion, while southward the Lomonds and Fife stand out.

It is not quite possible to see Dunsinane Hill, to where Macbeth's forces are supposed to have marched, using branches taken from Birnam as camouflage. One interesting point is that to retain the metre of the verse, Shakespeare has to have Dunsin*ane* pronounced with the stress on the last syllable, whereas locally it is said Dun*sin*ane. Leaving aside the problems of writing heroic blank verse, the view is well worth the effort of attaining it, and at least you know that from here it is all downhill!

Schiehallion from
Birnam Hill

Leave the summit and start walking quite steeply down. The path winds around in a contorted manner but is always quite clear. It crosses a flatter, wet area before descending again. There are a number of reassuring waymarkers. As if fed up with all the twisting about, the path finally gathers itself for a headlong plunge downhill through fine mixed woodland with some splendid old trees, including many birches. At the top of this final section there is a lovely view across Dunkeld and Birnam, with Loch of the Lowes to the right.

Please take great care on this descent, as it is very easy to slip, especially if the ground is wet. There is no need to hurry. The path leads directly to the foot of the hill where you turn right beside the Inchewan Burn to return to the station.

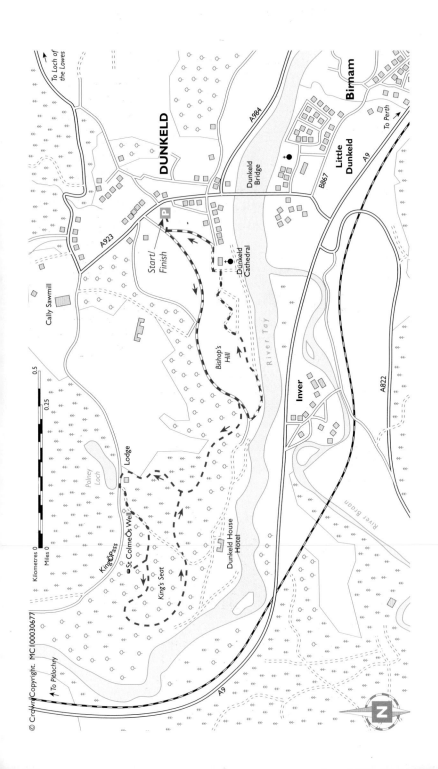

THE LARCH WALK

This walk is named for the fine trees first introduced to Scotland in this area over 200 years ago, but it has many other interesting features as well. It goes through part of the large estate now attached to Dunkeld House Hotel, currently owned by the Hilton Group and superbly placed beside the Tay.

From the car park, walk round the right-hand side of Stanley Hill and cross the grass half right to a gate giving access to the driveway of the hotel. Turn left and follow the drive (signposted Dunkeld Larches). It is better to walk on the grass verge rather than on the road.

The road runs alongside a large field which was the site of the original Dunkeld House, of which no trace now remains. It was here that in 1717, Rob Roy MacGregor was taken prisoner by the Duke of Atholl and then held briefly in Logierait Castle (see Walk 9). Across the field you have a fine view of Dunkeld Cathedral.

INFORMATION

Distance: 5.5km (3.5 miles).

Start and finish: North car park in Dunkeld (pay and display).

Terrain: Road, track and path. Some sections can be muddy in wet weather but special footwear is not usually needed.

Waymarked: Yes, with blue markers.

Refreshments: Wide choice in Dunkeld and at Dunkeld House Hotel. Toilets at the start.

Dunkeld House Hotel and Birnam Hill

Continue along the drive then, as the drive curves left before a right-hand bend, turn right onto a path signposted 'Duchesses Bridal Path'. This is one of a number of lovely old paths on the estate, laid out at a time when drives and viewpoints were created as much to impress visitors as for the pleasure of the owner, the Duke of Atholl. Note the intriguing plant-filled boat on the left!

The floral boat

The path stays level for a considerable time, contouring round the hill which falls away very steeply to the left down to the river. The path passes a seat and goes through rhododendron bushes, before making a big swing to the right. At this point the first tall old larches appear on either side. You are likely to see red squirrels in this area, which offers them a plentiful supply of food. You may also be startled by off-road vehicles which have a marked course around this area.

The path becomes broader and climbs to another waymarker. At a junction of tracks keep right, and then turn left to reach the edge of a field. Follow the track round several curves, keeping right at two junctions, almost to the lodge beside the road. Across the road at this point is Polney Loch and to the left is the King's Pass. This was the A9 before the bypass was made.

Turn left just before the lodge on a surfaced track, and after 200m go right on a path through a gate. In a further 300m turn right along a smaller path signposted to St Colme's Well, which is reached in 150m. The well is an attractive stone-arched spring with clear water bubbling out of it. The name Colm(e), otherwise Colman, Colum or Columba, is borne by over 200 saints, believe it or not, and there are many places in both Scotland and Ireland thought to have holy connections and named after one or other of these saints. There is a St Colman's Well at Fowlis, near Crieff. Bathing in or drinking from these wells was supposed to effect cures from all manner of ills.

St Colme's Well

Return to the main path and turn right, following the signpost for King's Seat, another very popular placename not always having a connection with any known king! The path emerges from the trees to give a superb view across the hotel buildings to the river and Birnam Hill — certainly a view fit for royalty.

Continue along the path, swinging left and going quite steeply downhill. The path runs parallel to a driveway and then joins it for 50m before you turn right onto a path which is also on the off-road route. After a T-junction turn right,

The Duchesses Bridal Path

climbing on a rough track, then going left and right on a better path.

Keep left round a clearing and at the next junction, turn right to re-join the outward route. Follow it almost back to the point where you left the drive, but this time turn right down steps to the drive. Cross, and in 80m turn left on a broad path through the trees with the river just below to your right.

Follow the path by the field edge all the way to the cathedral fence, then turn left to find the 'Parent Larch'. The first successful plant-ing of larches in this area was from seedlings brought back from the Tyrol, in Austria, by Colo-nel Menzies of Glen Lyon. He gave some of them to the 2nd Duke of Atholl, and five were planted here in 1738. Four have gone and this is the only survivor — a venerable tree indeed, which has seen a tremendous parade of Scottish history during its two and a half centuries of life.

Turn right to walk along a path at the field edge. You can then either go left to walk back round Stanley Hill, or right towards the cathedral gates, into Cathedral Street and back through the town to the car park.

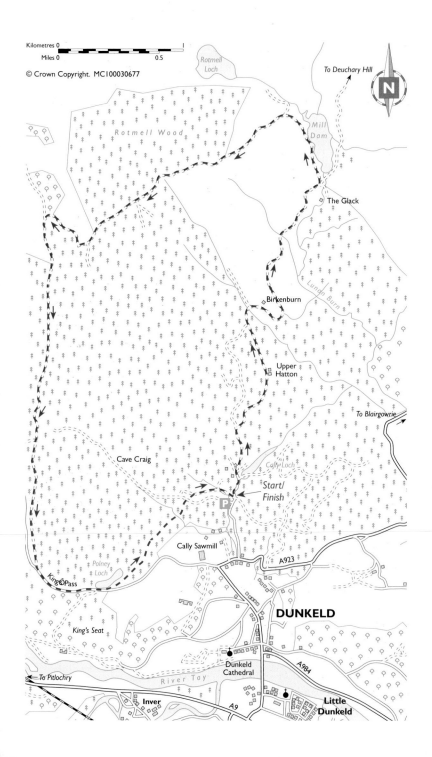

Kilometres 0 1
Miles 0 0.5

© Crown Copyright. MC100030677

Rotmell Loch

To Deuchary Hill

N

Rotmell Wood

Mill Dam

The Glack

Lunch Burn

Birkenburn

Upper Hatton

To Blairgowrie

Cave Craig

Cally Loch

Start/ Finish

P

Cally Sawmill

A923

Polney Loch

King's Pass

DUNKELD

King's Seat

To Pitlochry

Dunkeld Cathedral

A984

River Tay

Inver

A9

Little Dunkeld

MILL DAM

This is another very varied walk with good views along the way. From the car park, return to the track which you drove up and turn left. You may have noticed at the lodge that the track is signposted as a public footpath to Kirkmichael, 24km (15 miles) away. You are not going that far! The track is also signposted to a house called The Glack, and for the first part of the walk, all that is needed in route-finding is to keep following signs to The Glack (or the yellow waymarks).

The track climbs gently through mature woodland on the Atholl Estates. This is a working wood, and you can often hear the sawmill away to the left busy converting raw trunks and boughs into cut logs. Before too long, Cally Loch is passed, almost hidden in the trees down to the right. There are high crags away to the left. Continue with the track as it winds up and round to reach Upper Hatton, a beautifully modernised house. In the fields, cattle and horses may be grazing.

INFORMATION

Distance: 10km (6 miles).

Start and finish: The Cally car park. From Dunkeld, take the A923 Blairgowrie road and in 400m turn left at the lodge on a track. Go up the track for 500m and the car park is on the left.

Terrain: Tracks and paths. Parts of the walk can be muddy so strong footwear is advised.

Waymarked: Yes, yellow markers as Atholl Woods Walk.

Refreshments: Wide choice in Dunkeld.

Toilets: At car park in Dunkeld.

Mill Dam, a tranquil upland loch

The track twists right to pass below Birkenburn, crossing a burn by a fine old stone bridge, then heading left again with the views becoming more open. Deuchary Hill (509m) is clear ahead and the roofs of The Glack peep through the trees. The track continues climbing until The Glack is reached, 2.5km after leaving the car park. The houses command a fine view southwards.

Fork left before the houses through a gate to reach Mill Dam, a lovely upland loch. There are boats stored in the shed but the loch is no longer fished. This is a tranquil and very attractive spot with a number of good picnic places along its shore — an ideal lunch stop if you have timed it right. Birdlife here may include widgeon, mallard and tufted ducks.

Keep left of the loch and just past its northern end, where the main track swings sharply right, go left through a gate along a grassy track heading for a gap between heathery hills. Go through the gap, the going underfoot becoming more stony, to walk beside a forestry plantation, Rotmell Wood, with a fence on your right.

Mill Dam

There may be cattle along this stretch of track. In a further 400m, pass through a gate into the wood, which has a mixture of trees, mainly coniferous. Parts of it are being harvested for the timber. Keep straight on at the next junction, then go through another gate and continue, now with the wood to your left. The track descends towards the Tay Valley with Craigvinean Forest dominating the hill opposite and a fine northward view opening up.

Keep with the track as it swings sharply right then left, then turn left as waymarked along the broad track which runs straight across the hill. At the edge of the wood note the superb old 'granny' pine up to the left. There is also an ancient beech tree just beside the gate. Go through the gate and continue on the track, which can be rather muddy after rain. There is a marked contrast between the dense spruce plantation to the right and the much more open pinewood to the left.

Go through another gate by a small kissing gate at its side and continue along the track. The River Tay can be glimpsed through the trees, down below to the right, and the traffic on the A9 is usually audible. There is still a sense of freedom as you follow the track through the trees, going slightly downhill. Birdsong may include the high-pitched call of the woodpecker (or yaffle) and the plaintive mew of a buzzard circling overhead.

In a further kilometre, the track begins to drop more steadily. Go through another gate and continue downhill, passing banks of beautiful purple rhododendrons in spring. The track runs down to meet a road at a gate.

Continue along the road, walking on the verge. In 600 metres, leave the road on the left to walk beside the attractive Polney Loch, its surface a mass of water lilies. It has an almost secretive air about it and there is a temptation to linger. The loch is also known as the Goat Pool, and its situation, below the steep cliffs of Craig y Barns, is almost alpine in character. When you reach the end of the loch, go right through a gateway following a good path through mature conifer woodland.

Before long the big Cally Sawmill can be seen below to the right. This is a very busy place, with timber from the extensive woodlands in the area coming here to be processed into sawn lengths for building purposes or posts for fencing. The path continues above the sawmill, passing a truly ancient pine which will never be used for timber but left to age naturally and quietly where it stands.

A welcome seat from which to admire the loch

The noise of the sawmill gradually recedes as you continue along the path, climbing steadily to return to the car park at the end of a satisfying walk.

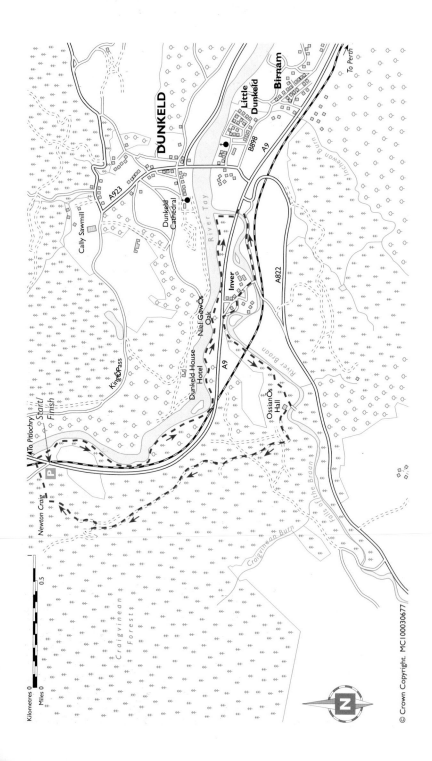

THE BANKS O' TAY

This very varied walk follows the banks of the Tay, visits Ossian's Hall, and passes through part of the large Craigvinean Forest. It provides a fine outing at any time of the year. From the car park, return to the road, cross it and go down the gravel path opposite. It passes under the railway on a 'creep' and then under the A9 bridge, which looks very impressive viewed from this unusual angle.

Continue along the bank of the Tay, a broad river here with both banks well wooded. The path runs along above the river and although the traffic on the A9 is clearly audible it does not spoil the pleasure of the walk. In about 500m, the path comes close to the railway. After a further 300m, where the river bends left, climb a short steep bank and continue on a broad path. After 200m the path begins to drop down to the river bank again, passing ruined buildings on the right.

At a fork, just past a waterpipe, go left, by the river. You are now opposite the grounds of the impressive Dunkeld House Hotel, with a fine view looking back upriver; in midstream is a small shingle island. Follow the path outside the field fence. Along here is Niel Gow's Tree, an oak named for the great fiddle-player who was born in 1727 at Inver. An unusual carved seat bears the inscription 'Sit beneath the fiddle tree with the ghost of Niel Gow next to me' (from a song by Michael Marra).

Continue beside the river, the path quite narrow at times. Cross the Inver mill stream and carry on, the path becoming broader as it passes beside a rather dark plantation. At a

INFORMATION

Distance: 8km (5 miles).

Start and finish: Newton Craig car park, reached by turning off the A9 just south of the bridge over the Tay on to the B898 road (signposted to Dalguise and Grandtully) and then turning left again immediately into the informal car park.

Terrain: Tracks and paths, some road. Strong footwear advised.

Waymarked: Yes, brown signs for Inver Walk.

Refreshments: Sometimes a snack bar in the Hermitage car park. Otherwise Dunkeld or Birnam.

Toilets: None on route. Nearest in Dunkeld.

Opening hours: The Hermitage: open all year, free.

The carved seat

The old bridge at Inver

junction, turn 90 degrees right to walk below power lines and then through another small wood.

Pass under the A9 again and cross the River Braan by a footbridge. Once over the river, which is less turbulent here than further upstream, turn sharp right along a tarmac path and in 100m go right again on a minor road (there is a pavement). Walk along beside the river and then Inver Mill caravan park.

Turn right over a lovely old bridge spanning the Braan, into the neat village of Inver with Forest Enterprise offices and workshops on the right. A house on the left sells its own honey. At the end of the road, turn left and walk beside the A9 for 200m before turning left and down a slope into The Hermitage car park.

Follow the main path from the car park beside the river, noting the many fine specimen trees. They include both Douglas and Silver Firs. The former tree is named after David Douglas, a noted botanist who discovered many new species and sent the first seeds of this fir back from North America in 1828. These trees were planted in 1919; in their native America they can grow to over 100m high.

Niel Gow's Oak

The Hermitage area was presented to the National Trust for Scotland in 1944 by Katharine, Duchess of Atholl, whose husband, the 8th Duke, was the Trust's first president. Marker posts show points of interest. At post 4 is an unusual multi-trunked beech, and at post 5 you can see across the river one of the tallest trees in Britain, a Douglas Fir over 65m high.

The track leads to Ossian's Hall, a folly built in 1758 overlooking the Falls of Braan, a series of rock steps over which the river crashes impressively (see Walk 12 for full details). When you leave the Hall, follow the path for 150m as far as post 8, then turn right on another path and then left along a broad track. This was the old turnpike road through Strathbraan. After 250m the track swings right and crosses another track. Go straight over on a forest road (blue cycleway signs).

After 250m the road narrows into a track. The track winds through Craigvinean Forest on a fairly level contour with a steep rocky slope to your left. In 1km turn very sharply right down another forest road and in 60m turn sharp left onto a grassy path.

This path leads down through mixed woodland to a small side valley which it follows to the right, descending quite steeply to reach a forest road. Turn right for a few metres to the car park where you started.

The banks of the Tay in summer

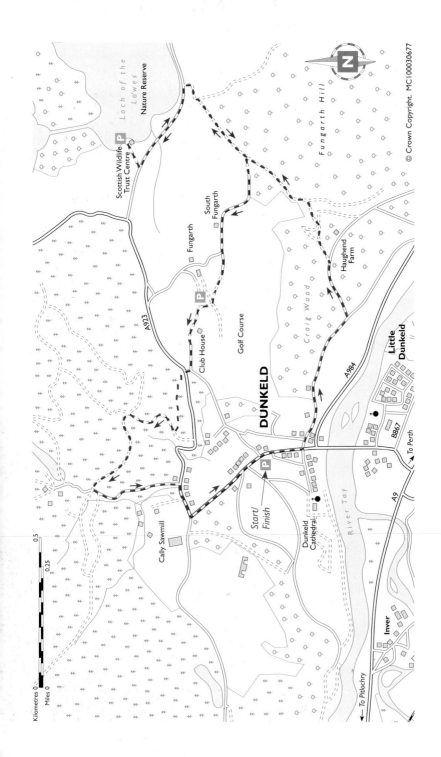

FUNGARTH AND LOCH OF THE LOWES

This walk rises to give excellent views before crossing farmland and passing through mature woods on the way back. An optional spur leads to the Scottish Wildlife Trust reserve at Loch of the Lowes. Leave the car park and turn right along the main street (see Walk 14 for details). Turn left up Brae Street which rises very steeply, passing Dunkeld Smoked Salmon, where you can buy their delicious products.

Continue up the steep brae, which eventually levels out, to your relief. After the houses end, the road becomes a narrow lane with little traffic. Pass a seat on the left and at the sign for Haughend, turn left along a track. Pass the entrance to Haughend Farm, beautifully set below a wooded slope, and continue uphill on the track through mature mixed woodland.

Go through a gateway and continue on the track. In a further 200m, at a gate where the track

INFORMATION

Distance: 8km (5 miles). 10km (6 miles) if spur is added.

Start and finish: The north car park in Dunkeld (pay and display).

Terrain: Roads, tracks and paths. Some sections can be muddy after wet weather, in which case strong footwear is advised.

Waymarked: Yes, with yellow signs.

Refreshments: Wide choice in Dunkeld.

Toilets: At car park in Dunkeld.

Livestock in the fields at Fungarth

continues to climb, leave it for a fenced path on the left, by the field edge. Follow this until it meets another track at a gate with a lovely view northwards over Fungarth. The track becomes stony and starts to descend. Another track comes in from the left. This is the eventual return route, but to see Loch of the Lowes, continue on a grassy path beside a dyke and then through a gate to meet a track. Turn left and walk down to the road.

Loch of the Lowes is a Scottish Wildlife Trust reserve which extends for 98ha and includes the fringe of surrounding woodland. The birdlife here is outstanding. The first Scottish breeding of great crested grebes was recorded here in 1870, and these lovely birds are still regular inhabitants. In winter the loch holds hundreds of greylag geese, but it is most famous for its breeding ospreys. First seen here in 1969, the 'fish eagles' have returned regularly since then.

The vibrant green of
Fungarth's hills

There is a small visitor centre with an observation hide at the north-west corner of the loch, which can be reached by going left along the road for about 500m. It is well worth a visit and with the powerful binoculars provided you have a very good chance of seeing the ospreys at their nest in spring. There are also many birds in the woodland fringing the loch, including woodpeckers, redstart, goldcrest and fly-catcher.

To continue the walk, return up the track and grassy path to the junction of tracks previously noted and turn right, then swing right and left round bends towards Fungarth. Go through a gate past South Fungarth, and at the next sharp right-hand bend go straight ahead through a gate on a fieldpath. Continue through two more gates to reach the edge of Dunkeld and Birnam golf course.

Keep to the right-hand side of the practice area and at its far corner, go up a path to cross the golf club car park and walk along the access road, taking the right fork. This road crosses a golf hole — look up to the left towards the tee and please heed the signs saying 'give way to golfers'. Just before the A923, go right on a boardwalk and path. Cross the road *with great care* and go up steps and left, along a path towards a dyke with a plantation beyond it. Follow the path through an area of fine old beech trees. The path parallels the A923 before swinging right to join a clear track through the plantation.

Fungarth

At a T-junction 250m further on, turn left. Go through a gate and into more open woodland, walking slightly downhill. At the broad main track, opposite the Cally car park, turn left and walk down to the A923. Turn right and follow the road down and then left back into Dunkeld.

The Loch of the Lowes

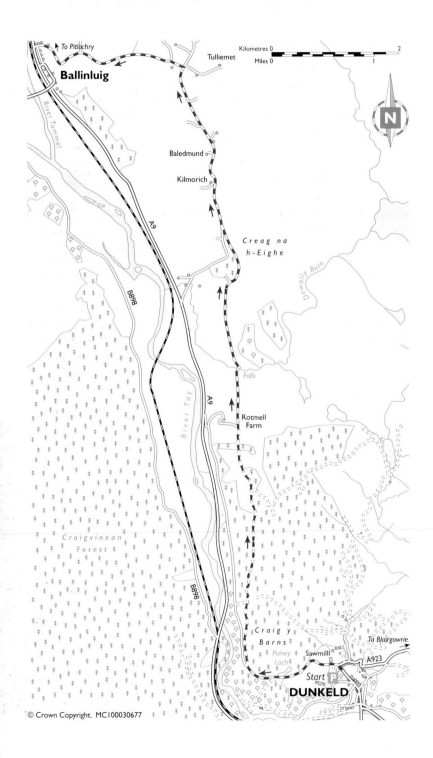

To Pitlochry

Ballinluig

Tulliemet

Kilometres 0 2
Miles 0 1

Baledmund

Kilmorich

A9

Creag na h-Eighe

B898

Dowally Burn

River Tummel

River Tay

Falls

Rotmell Farm

A9

Craigvinean Forest

B898

Craig y Barns

Polney Loch

Sawmill

To Blairgowrie

A923

Start

DUNKELD

© Crown Copyright. MC100030677

DUNKELD TO BALLINLUIG

This is one of the longer walks in the book, but it presents no difficulty and offers good views as you progress. It is a 'straight line' walk, with your destination in sight for much of the way, which you may regard as either good or bad according to your point of view!

From the car park in Dunkeld, turn left along the road and at the junction with the Blairgowrie road keep straight on, climbing past Cally Sawmill and a little further on, the peaceful reed-fringed Polney Loch. About 500m past the loch, leave the road and take the track climbing into the woods on the right. You now join, in reverse, part of the route of Walk 15.

The track climbs steadily through mixed, mainly coniferous woodland with the crags of Craig y Barns to the right and the busy A9 below to the left. Before long a fine view opens out across the valley to Craigvinean Forest and ahead towards Ballinluig.

INFORMATION

Distance: 14km (9 miles) linear.

Start: North car park, Dunkeld (pay and display).

Finish: Ballinluig. Return by bus—enquire locally for times.

Terrain: Roads and good tracks. Some sections can be muddy. Strong footwear advised, but take your trainers for the road sections.

Waymarked: No.

Refreshments: Pub and café at Ballinluig.

Toilets: At start and at pub or café in Ballinluig.

The track to Tulliemet

Ballinluig

After about 1km of steady climbing, the track levels out. I could find no sign of 'Willie Miller's Well' marked on the 1:25,000 map just right of the track here. Perhaps you will be luckier. Around here a thicker plantation on the left blocks the views for a while.

Leave the woods at a gate and continue along the track (the Mill Dam walk comes down from the right here). You can stride out along the track, which is broad and firm. The views open out again, and at the next gate, there is a particularly fine view of the Tay ahead and Ben Vrackie to the right.

The track stretches ahead, keeping to the same contour and passing through several gates. At the cross-tracks above Rotmell Farm, keep straight ahead, now walking between fields of sheep and cattle. Look down to the left and try to imagine the scene in January 1993, when this whole flat area from Ballinluig to Dunkeld was underwater as a result of serious flooding. A number of people had to be rescued by helicopter, but fortunately the flood warning system worked, and no lives either human or animal were lost.

The track dips a little to cross Dowally Burn by a fine old bridge. There are pretty tumbling falls to the right, but for much of the year they are rather hidden by the trees. The track briefly jinks left and right before resuming its straight-line progress through fields and small woods, often alive with pheasants which crash into the air in their clumsy, clattering way as you startle them.

The track enters a larger plantation with a belt of rhododendrons on the right separating you from open moorland. A clearing gives another splendid view up the Tay taking in Farragon Hill. On the right here is Creag na h-Eighe — 'the file crag', perhaps named from its sharp edges. The track, often rather muddy in this section, goes gently downhill and reaches the road at a gate by a house. Turn right here. At the next layby on the right, you could take the opportunity to switch from boots to trainers, the rest of the walk being on roads.

Before long, on the left, there is an appealing small memorial stone to Willie Birrell, who died at the age of 86 in 1995 and is 'sadly missed by his many friends'. His memory lives on at this lovely spot.

The Willie Birrell memorial

Walk past Kilmorich, possibly named for Muireadhach, one of the myriad Celtic saints (he died in 1011AD), and then Baledmund, which has the same name as the estate containing Ben Vrackie. *Bal* or *baile* is a steading, so this Edmund may have had two farms not far apart, each taking his name. Walk on to Tulliemet, where the road takes a sharp left-hand bend.

From here on it is steadily downhill, passing a fine beech wood on the right and an attractive pond on the left, before the road makes a double bend to reach the village of Ballinluig. Its name may mean 'steading of the bright stream', a reference either to the Tummel or perhaps even the wee burn you saw on the way down the hill. The inn is to the left, in the main street, and the café is just before it, by the garage.

The Ballinluig Inn

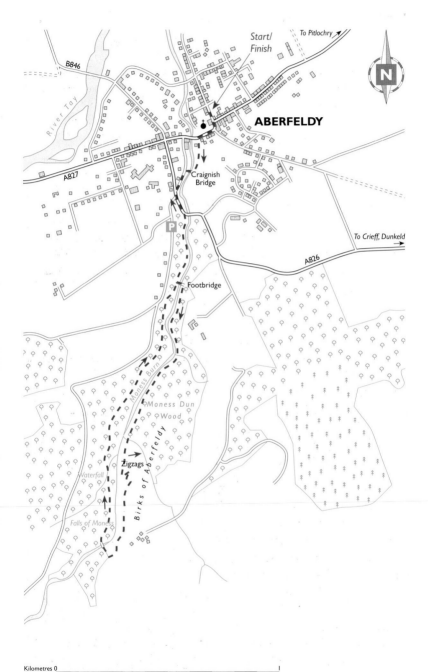

THE BIRKS OF ABERFELDY

The Birks is a popular walk with both locals and visitors, due both to the fine scenery and to the association with Scotland's national poet. Robert Burns is famous as a writer, but here we can consider him as an early conservationist too. He visited Aberfeldy in August 1787, took this walk, and wrote a song to mark the occasion. The fame of the Birks spread and the wooded glen of the Moness Burn has been carefully preserved ever since.

The walk starts in the Square in Aberfeldy, which has a fine ornamental fountain 'erected by Gavin, Marquis of Breadalbane, as a memento of the cordial reception accorded to him and Lady Breadalbane on their first visit after the restoration of the Marquisate, July 1885'. Walk west along the main street for a short distance and then turn left, following the blue sign to the Birks, to pass under the arch of the War Memorial, by neat Birks Cottage and along the path to reach and cross the Moness Burn at Craignish Bridge, originally erected through the generosity of Miss Jessica Campbell of Ericht House, Aberfeldy, in July 1914. The bridge was rebuilt in 1990.

Continue on the path beside the chuckling burn; in summer it is a lovely scene of dappled light and shade as the sun strikes through the trees, many of which are indeed birches. 'Birks' is a Scots word meaning either a single tree or a birchwood. The path crosses a lade (a man-made water channel, which feeds the working corn mill in Aberfeldy) and then goes up steps — the first of

INFORMATION

Distance: 6km (4 miles).

Start and finish: The Square, Aberfeldy. Car parking nearby.

Terrain: Good paths. Some steep climbing. The paths can be muddy after rain, and in such conditions strong footwear is advised.

Waymarked: Yes.

Refreshments: Wide choice in Aberfeldy.

Toilets: In Aberfeldy.

Side fall off Moness Burn

Sawara Cypress

many you will encounter on this walk — to meet the Crieff Road at a gate. Cross with care and walk up the track to a car park, passing some fine specimen trees. You can start the walk from here but I find it more satisfying to do the full trip from the town centre.

An information board describes the Birks and gives the words of Burns' famous song, the last quatrain of which runs:

> The braes ascend like lofty wa's,
> The foaming stream deep-roaring fa's,
> O'erhung wi' frequent spreading shaws,
> The Birks of Aberfeldy.

You can assess for yourself the accuracy of the poet's description as you continue the walk past a fine Japanese Cedar. There are leaflets in a box here; they describe the walk and are keyed to the numbered posts you will pass.

Where the path divides, go left, following the sign to the Moness Falls. Moness means 'the foot of the falls', and straightaway you cross a bridge below a small fall. The path climbs a little, then drops down to pass beside the burn, which here runs over smooth, water-worn rock. The Moness Burn, incidentally, was originally called the Pheallaidh (Feldy) Burn, from which the town took its name.

The Moness Falls

The path starts to climb in earnest, and for a time is fenced on the right. Small bridges take you over minor burns feeding into the main stream. It is easy to slip into a reverie along here and imagine yourself back in Burns' time, wandering through the 'spreading shaws' (a shaw is a small wood).

Continue following the path. The glen is becoming much more gorge-like, with sheer crags on the opposite bank. The path climbs a steep flight of wooden steps and crosses a bridge with a crag to the left. More steps lead to Burns' Seat, where the poet is said to have rested and gained the inspiration for his song. Perhaps if you sit here you too will be blessed with inspiration: the surroundings certainly encourage poetic thought.

Yet more steps, stone this time, lead up beside a fine waterslide and then back to cross the burn above the slide, still with falls on the left. Cross a long wooden bridge; the steep slope opposite has fine trees and a number of dead ones as well. A short spur path leads down to a viewing platform for the Moness Falls, a very impressive sight as the burn tumbles down between high crags.

There is still a fair amount of climbing to be done. Return to the main path and continue upward on more steps. The path turns back right and continues zig-zagging upward for some time to reach a point with a fine view of the upper falls — and the bridge that crosses them. The path curves right and gives a great view right back down the gorge to distant hills, then continues to the bridge over the falls. Below your feet the water leaps, and as Burns says, 'deep-roaring falls' over the lip.

After one last short climb the long descent begins. Partway down there is a superb view of Ben Vrackie. Other views are frustratingly obscured by foliage. In some ways this walk is very suitable for winter, when the trees are bare, the views are better, and the falls are often full. The path can however be tricky in frosty conditions.

The return path is perhaps of less interest than the outward route but it is still very pleasant to wander along through the lovely birches, back to the car park. Here you can enjoy the intriguing Tree Trail, which takes you in rapid succession past a host of unusual trees including Kashmiri Whitebeam, Antarctic Beech, Himalayan Birch, the Angelica or Devil's Walking Stick and a Chinese Scarlet Rowan, before you re-cross the road and walk back down to the town centre.

Ornamental fountain, Aberfeldy

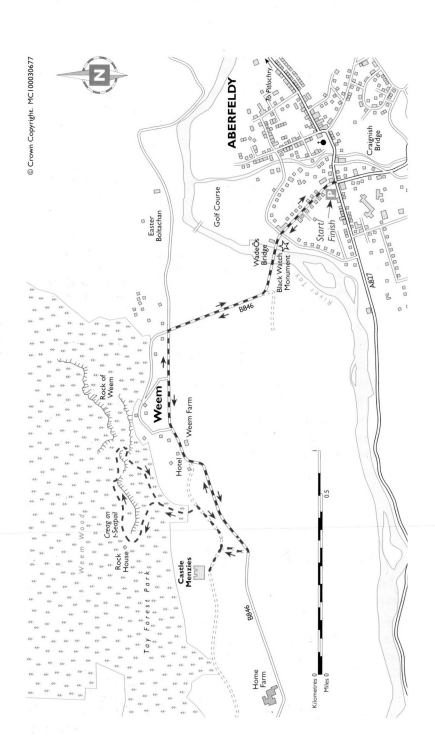

© Crown Copyright. MC100030677

WEEM WOODS AND CASTLE MENZIES

This walk extends out from the edge of Aberfeldy to the village of Weem and Castle Menzies, and includes a wonderful little walk in Weem Woods. It is of course perfectly possible to drive to the castle, but it is very satisfying to arrive on foot.

Start by viewing the large and imposing Black Watch Monument. Unveiled in November 1887 by the Marquis of Breadalbane, the monument depicts Private Farquhar Shaw wearing the original regimental uniform. Its cost of around £500 was raised by public subscription. The Black Watch (*Freiceadan Dubh* in Gaelic) was first raised in 1667 by clan chiefs on the order of King George II to keep the peace in the Highlands, and takes its name from the dark tartan it wore. The regiment was given the freedom of Aberfeldy in 1970.

From the green below the monument there is a superb view of Wade's Bridge over the Tay. Built as part of the military road between Stirling and Inverness, it was constructed in a single season between spring and autumn 1733 at a cost of

INFORMATION

Distance: 8km (5 miles).

Start and finish: Wade's Bridge, Aberfeldy. It is usually possible to park in Taybridge Drive, near the bridge.

Terrain: Roads and good path to St David's Well. No special footwear needed.

Refreshments: Wide choice in Aberfeldy. Tearoom at Castle Menzies.

Toilets: In Aberfeldy and at the castle.

Opening Hours: Castle Menzies: Apr-mid Oct, Mon-Sat 1030-1700. Sun 1400-1700 (tearoom Mon-Sat 1100-1630, Sun 1400-1630).

Wade's Bridge

The Black Watch Monument

£4,095 — easily the most expensive single project in the whole military road network and a magnificent achievement for its time. Although the lovely five-span bridge with its four tapering pillars is always associated with General Wade, it was actually designed by the famous architect William Adam; it is founded on 1200 wooden piles shod with iron.

Cross the bridge (with care — the footway is very narrow) and note the plaque on the first pillar on the right stating that Wade laid the first stone on 23 April 1733. During its construction, the old soldier complained that 'the Justices of Peace promised to furnish carriages for materials at the county's expense, but did not perform it'. He also said that '200 artificers and labourers from the army were employed for nearly a whole year'. They did well: after 270 years and innumerable raging floods on the Tay the old bridge is as solid as ever. Looking right, you can see an intriguing modern parallel: the world's first fibreglass bridge, built in 1992 to link the two halves of the golf course.

Continue along the road. Today it swings right, but the original line as engineered by Wade went straight on. When the pavement ends, cross and walk on the right facing the traffic. At the junction (where there was formerly a tollhouse), swing left to pass the Aileen Chraggan Hotel and reach the village of Weem. The name is a phonetic anglicising of the Gaelic *uamh*, meaning 'a cave', and there are indeed caves in the steep wood above.

Weem has two churches. Beside the present building is the Old Kirk of Weem. The building dates from the late 15th century (though it was much altered in the 17th century, as can be seen by the date 1614 on the roof cornerstones), and is dedicated to St Cuthbert, Bishop of Lindisfarne in the 7th century, who is said to have lived as a hermit in the woods here. There was a church of some sort in Weem as far back as 1235. In 1839 the Old Kirk was dedicated by Sir Neil Menzies as a mausoleum for his family and clan, and today it contains many fascinating relics including the huge stone Menzies Monument and two ancient stone crosses taken from a long-disused monastery at Dull. If the kirk is not open, the key can be obtained from Clematis Cottage nearby.

Weem Rock

Continue past the Weem Hotel, with its portrait of General Wade on the outside wall. He used the building as his base during the construction of the bridge and road in 1733. Continue along the road for 400m (there is a pavement) to the

Weem's two kirks

entry to Castle Menzies and turn right. At the fork go right for the woodland walk to St David's Well. The car park contains two large carved stone tables, one relating to St Cuthbert, the other bearing the inscription: 'deep in the ancient wood of Weem amid brooding rocks and hidden caves, dragons and demons in legend dwell'.

Continue into the wood, following red waymarks. This must be one of the best short walks anywhere in Scotland, and besides the dragons and demons (the more vivid your imagination, the better) is a superb example of path engineering. At first you twist steeply uphill. At a junction go ahead; the path swerves this way and that, as if its builders were being chased by demons. At a fork go left, climbing stone steps which look old but aren't, to reach the top of Weem Rock with its fine view.

Castle Menzies

There are more steps and then, as if tired of climbing, the path runs across the foot of a line of huge crags, in one of which is the well ascribed to St David. This should probably be *Sir* David (Menzies), who in 1440 renounced the world and took holy orders. St Cuthbert is also said to have sheltered here. The overhang forms a sort of cave, from which the village below perhaps took its name.

The path starts to descend, passing below more frowning crags, then briefly climbs, dips and swerves before finally settling on a return route at an interpretation board for Ancient Woodland. You cross the wood at a lower level before returning to the fork and retracing the outward route back to the car park. Walk back along the access track and turn right to reach Castle Menzies.

Castle Menzies

Weem has been the home of the Menzies family since at least the 14th century, and the castle is a fine example of a fortified house. It was inherited by the Clan Menzies Society in 1957 in a dilapidated condition. Since then a great deal of restoration has been carried out and an extensive tour of the older part of the castle is now offered. A full guide and other interesting material is available at the reception desk. Bonnie Prince Charlie stayed in the castle in February 1746 on his way north to the fateful end to his campaign at Culloden; shortly afterwards his eventual conqueror, 'Butcher' Cumberland, was also here.

After visiting the castle, return by the same route through the village and back over Wade's Bridge. Before leaving Aberfeldy it is worth visiting the watermill, which is still working. The huge wheel is a very impressive sight when in operation.

Elaborate stonework at the entrance to Castle Menzies

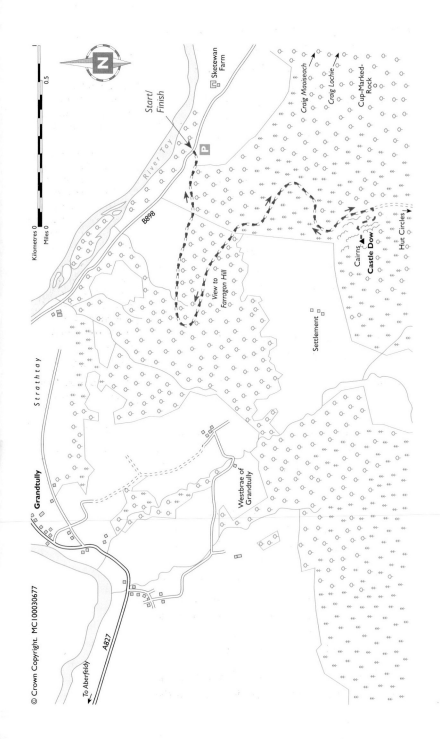

© Crown Copyright. MC100030677

CASTLE DOW

This short walk leads to a hilltop decorated with unusual 'stone man' cairns which is a magnificent viewpoint, and is worth saving for a clear day. Go up the track and through a gate, climbing steadily through mixed broadleaved woodland with many fine birch and rowan. You may be lucky enough to see deer in the wood.

After 1km the track turns sharply back to the left and continues to climb. A particularly good view opens out behind you, its central feature Farragon Hill above Aberfeldy with its 'cottage loaf' upper section. Through a gate and before a double bend there is a fine view in the other direction through the birch trees, taking in the river and its strath. Continue, noting that the upper part of the wood above you is now a conifer plantation. You may well see buzzards in this area, and perhaps hear their distinctive mewing cry.

Go through another gate. At one time the bald top of Castle Dow was clearly seen ahead from this point, with the 'stone men' standing out. However, the tree growth now means that it is obscured, and remains hidden for a while longer. Continue along the track round the left side of the hill, still climbing steadily.

At a small cairn beside the track, take the clear path going up to the right. Over to the left is the open moorland of Craig Maoiseach and Craig Lochie. This whole area is full of ancient field systems, hut circles and signs of settlement dating back thousands of years, which archaeologists are still investigating. Meet and follow a stone dyke. Continue beside the dyke to the top of the hill, cross the dyke at a gap and walk across to the cairns.

The effort of getting here is rewarded both by the intriguing collection of tall, slender cairns on the

INFORMATION

Distance: 6km (4 miles).

Start and finish: There is no formal parking at the start of this walk, but two or three cars can be accommodated. The start is 250m past the farm of Sketewan, on the B898 road east of Grandtully, where a forest road emerges. The grid reference is 934524.

Terrain: Good track, short section of path and open hill. The walk is straightforward and presents no difficulty. No special footwear needed.

Waymarked: No.

Refreshments: None en route. Nearest at Grandtully.

Toilets: None on route.

Above and below: the 'stone man' cairns

summit and by the view. There are about a dozen cairns, but it is not clear whether they are laid out in a pattern. The name Castle Dow probably comes from the Gaelic *caisteal dubh*, the black castle. There are remains of an ancient fort, 90m by 65m, walled and with additional ramparts. Its strategic importance in terms of the views it commands are obvious.

The view is indeed breathtaking. To the west is the distinctive cone of Schiehallion, the 'fairy hill of the Caledonians', and the long line of hills running either side of Glen Lyon. To the north-east, Ben Vrackie is clear, and below you are the shapely curves of the Tay. Across the valley, Farragon Hill again stands out. It is a place to linger and savour to the full.

The return journey to the car park is made by the same route, enjoying the views in the opposite direction, and also the fact that it is all downhill. I hope you will agree that it was worth taking this walk to savour a hilltop with a very special atmosphere and a superb panorama of Highland Perthshire.

Above: Farragon Hill from Castle Dow

Below: Strathtay from below Castle Dow

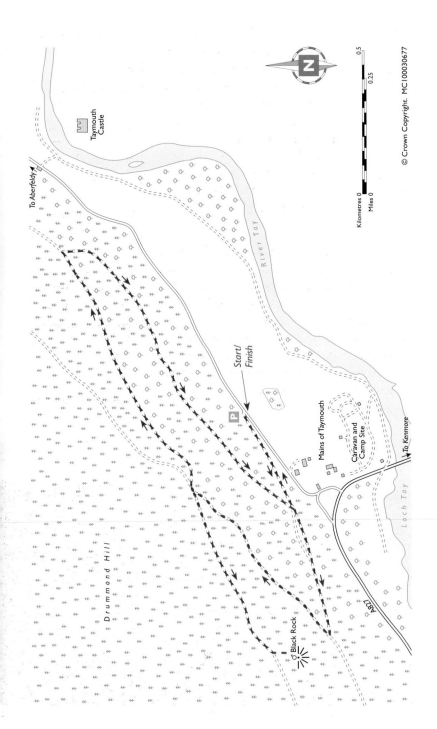

To Aberfeldy

Taymouth
Castle

River Tay

Start/
Finish

P

Mains of Taymouth

Caravan and
Camp Site

Loch Tay

To Kenmore

Drummond Hill

Black Rock

A827

Kilometres 0
Miles 0

0.25

0.5

© Crown Copyright. MC100030677

DRUMMOND HILL

D rummond Hill is said to be Scotland's oldest managed forest, and was first designed and planted by Black Duncan, laird of Breadalbane, in the 17th century. It was one of the Forestry Commission's first purchases after the Commission was established in 1919 as a response to timber shortages experienced after the ravages of World War One, and has been managed for timber production ever since. The forest now has two walking routes and is also used for orienteering competitions and car rallies on occasion.

From the car park, follow the wide track steadily uphill for 800m with occasional views of Kenmore and Loch Tay to the left. At a junction, turn sharply right and continue climbing for a further kilometre. The forest contains trees of mixed age and maturity, with a variety of species including Scots pine, Norway and Sitka spruce and Douglas fir. Felling and replanting has taken place throughout the past 80 years and continues today.

INFORMATION

Distance: 6km (4 miles).

Start and finish: Drummond Hill car park. Turn east off A827 at Kenmore on minor road and after 600m turn left as signposted. The car park is 200m up the track.

Terrain: Good forest tracks and paths. No special footwear needed.

Waymarked: Yes, blue and red markers.

Toilets: In Kenmore.

Refreshments: None en route. Good selection in Kenmore.

Kenmore from Drummond Hill

Loch Tay and Drummond Hill

Drummond Hill is one of the forests where the capercaillie, Scotland's largest game bird, is found. After becoming extinct in Britain in the late 18th century due to over-hunting and forest clearance, the bird was reintroduced here from Sweden in 1837. It is often heard before it is seen as it crashes noisily through the forest understorey.

At the next junction, turn left (blue waymark for the viewpoint) and continue along another track, climbing slightly for 1km before levelling out and then turning left along a short path off the track to the Black Rock viewpoint. From here you look down on Loch Tay and Kenmore and across the loch to the hills on its south side. From Kenmore, the River Tay, which has the largest catchment area of any river in Britain at nearly 5000 km², starts its journey towards the sea at Dundee. The Tay regularly floods and in January 1993 it and its sister rivers caused extensive flooding over a very wide area from Aberfeldy to Perth. During that flood, the peak flow of over 2200 cubic metres per second (equivalent to half a million gallons of water *every second*) was the greatest ever recorded in Britain.

From the viewpoint, return down the track to the junction and take the right fork with the red waymarkers. Through the trees you can glimpse Taymouth Castle and its golf course. The castle, which incorporates an older 16th century building, largely dates from the 19th century, but has been unused for some time. Further on there is a fine view of the Tay as it swings sinuously round a bend, often with foaming white rapids, and a little further on again, a superb view of the whole strath with the river winding through woods and farmland towards Aberfeldy.

At a turning circle on the track, 1km after the junction, turn right (look carefully for the waymark) down a small path, and immediately fork right. Just when you thought you had finished climbing, it goes up again! It soon levels out and then winds through pleasant mixed woodland often alive with birdsong. There are two or three more short climbs along this stretch.

The path levels out and crosses a gully where a wooden rail has been erected as a guard following a landslip, always likely to happen on slopes such as this in periods of heavy rain. It seems as if the path is never going to end, but eventually you see the forest track below and the path drops down to join it 200m above the car park—and I bet you didn't see the path turn-off on the way up! It is indeed well hidden.

Return to the car park at the end of another enjoyable walk.

Taymouth Castle and golf course

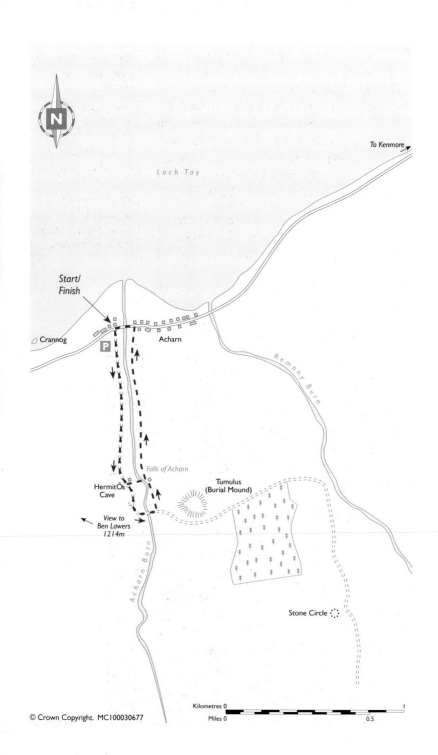

THE FALLS OF ACHARN

This is one of the most delightful short walks to be found anywhere, and is ideal for a summer evening or a fine day when you have a couple of hours to spare. To reach the start, drive along the minor road on the south side of Loch Tay from Kenmore for about 2km, and on reaching Acharn cross a neat stone bridge and park tidily on the verge opposite the shop. A sign points up the track towards the falls.

Follow the track, climbing steadily past a farm and two houses. This track is occasionally used by large agricultural vehicles extracting timber so be prepared to give way if one comes up or down.

INFORMATION

Distance: 4 km (2.5 miles).

Start and finish: Acharn village, 3km west of Kenmore.

Terrain: Good tracks and paths. No special footwear needed.

Waymarked: Yes.

Refreshments: None en route. Good choice in Kenmore.

The Falls of Acharn

Another view of the falls

After the initial climb, the track levels off, giving a fine view back over Loch Tay to the forested Drummond Hill (walk 23). The Acharn Burn can be heard rushing down on your left. Opposite a fieldgate, a short signposted path to the left leads to the Hermit's Cave, a corbelled stone viewing chamber for the lower falls set into this side of the gorge. It looks very dark inside but don't be afraid to go in; there is a fireplace and seats, and a short curving tunnel leads to a balcony giving a lovely view of the falls.

Continue a little further along the track, climbing again, until, round a double bend, a sign points left down a path to a viewing platform. The platform and footbridge were built by 202 Field Squadron RE in June 1989 and give a superb view of the upper Falls of Acharn. To the right, the water thunders down over three rock lips, leaping and crashing from one to another, and then swirls down a long waterslide over the rock beneath the bridge before tumbling sideways over another rock lip to the lower falls below. It is a very impressive place, especially after a period of rain when the falls are well fed with water.

When you are ready to continue, return to the track and continue upwards for a short way to the point where the burn is crossed by a fine old stone bridge. From just before the bridge you can enjoy the view along the loch in both directions, and look over to the grand hills on either side, which include, on the north of the loch, Ben Lawers, at 1214m (3986ft) the highest hill in Perthshire. It is part of a national nature reserve and is owned by the National Trust for Scotland.

When you have enjoyed the view to the full, cross the bridge over the burn and on the far side, turn left through a kissing gate on to a path, which leads to another very fine view of the falls from under spreading beech trees — a lovely spot to tarry a while on a fine day.

Continue downhill on the path, passing the foot-bridge and viewing platform (if you can—another look is very tempting); a little further on a seat gives a grand view across to the Hermit's Cave. The burn has now crashed over the long lower fall and is a considerable distance below in its gorge.

Continue down beside a stone dyke and then a fence, dropping steadily towards the village. Past a small hut beside a buried water tank, the path becomes a clear track leading easily down past two more stone water authority buildings. Pass a children's playground and walk through an attractive group of houses to the road. Turn left over the bridge for a few metres back to the start of the walk.

Loch Tay in summer

Acharn is another place with Rob Roy MacGregor connections. During the 1716-18 period, when he was a hunted man following the failure of the 1715 Jacobite Rising, which he strongly supported, some of Rob's children stayed in Acharn and went to school here. He had relatives at Taymouth and the children were sent here to be safe. Rob's own homes, first in Glen Dochart and then on Loch Lomondside, were burnt by government forces during this troubled period.

While in Acharn you can also visit an intriguing herb garden which has a range of produce for sale, and on the way back to Kenmore it is worth stopping at the Scottish Crannog Centre, where you can see a reconstruction of a crannog, a lake dwelling once quite common in Scotland.

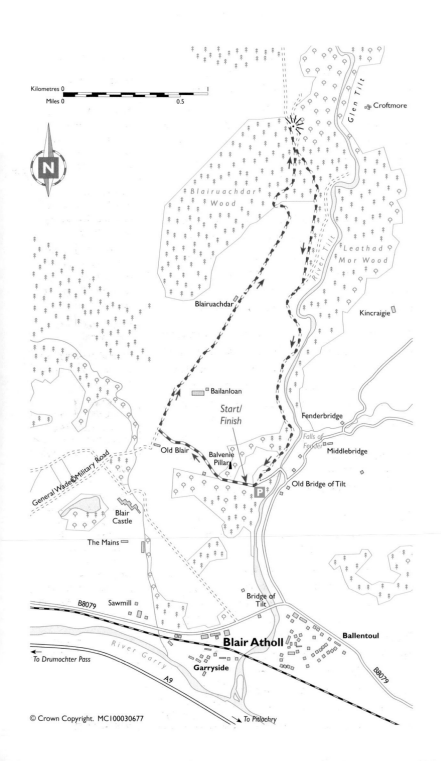

Kilometres 0   1
Miles 0   0.5

N

Croftmore

Glen Tilt

Blairuachdar Wood

Leathad Mor Wood

River Tilt

Blairuachdar

Kincraigie

Bailanloan

Start/ Finish

Fenderbridge

Falls of Fender

Old Blair

Middlebridge

Balvenie Pillar

Old Bridge of Tilt

General Wade Military Road

Blair Castle

The Mains

B8079

Sawmill

Bridge of Tilt

Ballentoul

Blair Atholl

River Garry

To Drumochter Pass

Garryside

A9

B8079

To Pitlochry

© Crown Copyright. MC100030677

GLEN TILT

Atholl Estates own and manage a huge area extending to nearly 60,000 hectares, mainly stretching north and east from the village of Blair Atholl. The estates have laid out a number of waymarked walks in the area around Blair Castle and lower Glen Tilt, and the route followed here uses one of them. A booklet giving details of all the walks is available from local outlets, price £1.00.

From the car park, walk back up to the junction and turn left on the road. In about 250 metres, opposite the farm entrance, go right at the sign for the Balvenie Pillar. Climb the stone steps and continue on the path zig-zagging up the hill and then alongside a fence to reach the pillar.

The pillar, a tapering obelisk about 10m high, was erected in 1755 by the 2nd Duke of Atholl on this hill, known as Tom na Cruiche (Hangman's Knoll), to mark the site of the last public hanging in the area, in 1630. The view westwards extends to the unmistakable cone of Schiehallion, while in the foreground below you is a statue of Hercules in the castle grounds. The statue, copied from a Roman original, was carved by John Cheere in 1743 and cost just £25.

Return to the road and turn right. As the road swings left, if you look back you can see the Pillar at the edge of the trees. There may be Highland cattle, with their distinctive horns, in the fields here. This road was the coaching route from Perth to Inverness before the modern road was built. At a crossroads, turn right on the road past the Home Farm (named as Bailanloan on OS maps). In former times, the farm would have supplied the

The Balvenie Pillar

INFORMATION

Distance: 8km (5 miles).

Start and finish: Car park, Old Bridge of Tilt. From the south end of Blair Atholl, take the minor road signed to Old Blair, turn left over the River Tilt and the car park is 200m further on, on the left.

Terrain: Good paths and tracks. Boots or strong shoes recommended in wet conditions.

Waymarked: Yes, green arrows.

Refreshments: None en route. Good choice in Blair Atholl.

Opening Hours: Blair Castle: Easter-end October, daily, 10.00-17.00, admission charge. The Atholl Estates Information Centre, opposite the main entrance to the castle, has displays on the management of the estate and other information such as the guided walks programme. It is also the base for the estate Ranger service. The centre is open from Easter to October (tel. 01796 481646).

Double bridge over the
Banvie Burn

provisions for the castle and estate, but it is now
largely a livestock farm rearing sheep and cattle
for sale at market.

The road climbs steadily and becomes a little
rougher. There is a fine view back across the wider
glen, while below to the right is Glen Tilt, your
return route. Continue past the buildings at
Blairuachdan, after which the road becomes a track
and enters woodland. The track swings sharp left
and right to cross a burn. At a junction go straight
on. At the next fork keep right, slightly downhill.
In 100 metres notice the marker pointing down-

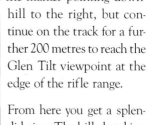

hill to the right, but continue on the track for a further 200 metres to reach the
Glen Tilt viewpoint at the
edge of the rifle range.

From here you get a splendid view. The hill ahead is a
Munro, Carn a' Chlamain
('hill of the buzzard', 983m).
This was one of many hills
climbed by Queen Victoria
in her younger days, and in

Carn a' Chlamain and
Glen Tilt

her diary for 21 September 1844 she recorded that
"Lady Cumming, Lord Glenlyon and I went up
quite to the top, which is deep in moss. The view
was quite beautiful, nothing but mountains all
around us, and the solitude, the complete solitude,
very impressive." So it is today, Ma'am.

Glen Tilt is a superb through walk on one of the
classic foot journeys in Scotland, leading in time either to the Lairig Ghru and Aviemore, or by turning
right, the River Dee and Braemar. This however is a
two-day expedition. Our present aspirations are more
modest, but it is still satisfying to look up the glen
from this point and take in the lovely view.

Retrace your steps to the marker and turn left
down the grassy path, beside a plantation fence.

Blair Castle

In time you enter a birch wood. Birch was a very useful wood in former times, used for making utensils such as bowls, while the smaller branches and saplings were used for bedding.

The path descends steadily to meet the main Glen Tilt track, which is followed for the final part of the walk. The River Tilt can be heard and occasionally seen below to the left, tumbling over rocks in its haste to join the Garry. The track goes through a mixture of fields and woodland to return you eventually to the car park.

Before or after your walk you might like to visit Blair Castle, the very impressive home of the Dukes of Atholl. The earliest parts date back to the 13th century, but much of what you see today is 18th century. You can also, for a small fee, visit the extensive gardens and policies around the castle, including the Diana Grove, the Hercules Garden and St Bride's, the old parish church where John Graham of Claverhouse, 'Bonnie Dundee', was brought to be buried after the Battle of Killiecrankie in 1689.

Highland cattle may be seen
on this walk

© Crown Copyright. MC100030677

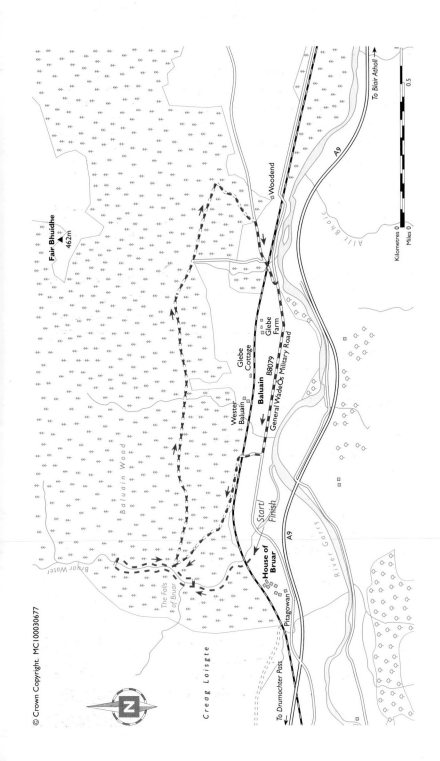

THE FALLS OF BRUAR

The renowned Falls of Bruar make a superb short walk. An extension giving a longer outing is also described. The walk starts and finishes at the House of Bruar, which has a full range of shops, restaurant, toilets and other visitor facilities. The Clan Donnachaidh Museum is on the same site.

From the lower car park, follow the sign past the Heather and Alpine Nursery and turn left on the path beside the Bruar Water. Pass through a gate to the right of Bruar Lodge and continue, passing under the railway by a low tunnel and through another gate. There are already beginnings of an impressive gorge to the right.

The path climbs steadily to reach the Lower Falls at a picturesque bridge. Early visitors to the falls found a propsect of bare open moorland. The poet Robert Burns was so moved by the lack of trees that in 1787 he addressed a poem, *The Humble Petition of Bruar Water*, to the Duke of Atholl. Its full 11 verses can be found in the walks leaflet obtainable near the start, but the main plea is:

> Would then my noble master please to
> grant my highest wishes?
> He'll shade my banks wi' tow'ring trees and
> bonnie spreading bushes.
> Delighted doubly then, my Lord, you'll
> wander on my banks
> And listen many a grateful bird return you
> tuneful thanks.

The Duke took due notice and planted the area with larch and pine. None of the original trees remain but the area has continued to be wooded, and most visitors would agree that the effect is a great benefit to the scene.

INFORMATION

Distance: 7km (4.5 miles) or 2km (1.3 miles) short option.

Start and finish: House of Bruar, signposted from A9 5km north of Blair Atholl.

Terrain: Good paths, tracks and road. Some rocky sections. Boots or strong shoes recommended.

Waymarked: Partly.

Toilets: At the start.

Refreshments: At the House of Bruar.

The path to the upper bridge

Looking down from the upper bridge

The little stone arch by the bridge was originally part of a 'viewing house' of which there were several, provided to give visitors the most 'picturesque' experience. However, not everybody approved of the rather formal layout. Visiting in 1803, William Wordsworth found the paths, 'brushed neatly without a blade of grass or a weed upon them', quite out of character. The path now has a more natural appearance.

Continue climbing through fine trees, with rhododendrons providing a display of colour in spring and early summer. The river is hidden for a while but still clearly audible, despite being a long way below.

Reach the Upper Bridge and cross it. There is a grand view in both directions. The falls are naturally at their best after rain, when a thunderous torrent rushes down the gorge. Burns charmingly described this as 'foaming down the skelvy rocks' and said it was 'worth gaun' a mile to see'. Many have travelled rather further than that!

On the south bank there is a small picnic area, and the return path starts here. Follow the path down the lip of the gorge, the river again heard but not seen, to a point where a broad track comes in from the left (at a seat with a superb view back to the main falls). You have a choice of routes here. For the short walk, simply continue through the gate and down beside the river (for a description see later in the text). For the longer walk, take the upper track.

It runs almost level through fine mature woodland of pine, spruce and larch and provides pleasant and easy walking. After about a kilometre, the views start to open out to include the surrounding hills.

After another kilometre, pass a field on the right and then, with the track descending gently beside a plantation to a gate passed by a steep ladder stile, reach a junction of tracks. Turn right here and continue downhill round several bends to another junction.

Turn right again (a red waymarker points left) and follow the track over the railway by a fine old bridge and down to the road at the lodge house. Exit by the gate on the right, marked for the use of walkers and cyclists.

Walk along the road for about a kilometre and then, about 150 metres before the large road sign, turn right on a track, pass under the railway and turn left. Go through a gate and continue with the track, climbing steadily to return to the viewpoint you left earlier on.

Turn left here, through the gate, and continue with the path by the river to the lower bridge. There was originally another 'viewing house' by the lower path near the gate but all trace of it is now gone. Cross the lower bridge, again admiring the view of the falls, and follow the outward path back to the House of Bruar.

The natural rock arch

INDEX

Aberfeldy 35, 79-81, 83-87
Acharn 97-99
Adam, William 84
Albert, Prince 21
Allean Forest 41-43
Allt Lochan nan Losguinn 43
An Suidhe 34
Ardtulichan 15
Atholl, Dukes of 38, 47, 59-61, 68, 101, 103, 105
Atholl Estates 63, 101
Atholl Memorial Fountain, Dunkeld 47
Atholl Monument, Logierait 38
Atholl Palace Hotel 27, 37

Bailanloan 101
Baledmund 77
Balfour Stone 2
Ballinluig 37, 75-77
Balrobbie 16
Balvenie Pillar 101
Barbour, Dr 6
Barbour, Helen 12
Beatrix Potter Garden 45, 46
Beinn Eagagach 42
Beinn a' Ghlo 6, 10, 15, 20, 25
Ben Lawers 99
Ben Vrackie 7, 10, 13, 15, 19-21, 27, 38, 39, 76, 81, 93
Birkenburn 63
Birks of Aberfeldy 79-81
Birnam 45-47, 49
    Hill 55-57
    Institute 46
    Oak 45
Birnham Burn 56
Birrell, Willie 77
Black Spout waterfall 27-29
Black Watch 83
Black Duncan 93
Black Rock viewpoint 94
Blair Atholl 2, 24, 101-103
Blair Castle 16, 103
Blairuachdan 102

'Bonnie Dundee' 2, 103
Bonnie Prince Charlie 87
Breadalbane, Marquis of 79, 81
Bruar 105-107
Burns, Robert 79-81, 105, 106
Butter family 37

Cairngorm Investments 47
Cally Loch 63
Cally Sawmill 65, 75
Campbell, Miss Jessica 79
capercaillie 94
Carn a' Chlamain 102
Carn Liath 2, 6, 10, 20
Castle Dow 89-91
Castle Menzies 83-87
Caulfeild, Major 51
Cheere, John 101
Clachan an Diridh 33
Clan Donnachaidh Museum 105
Clan Menzies 87
Clunie footbridge 6
Clunie Power Station 1, 2, 7
Clunie Walk 31
Colivoulin 28
Corhulichan 16
Coronation Bridge 7
Craig, Dr Robert 12
Craig Lochie 89
Craig Maoiseach 89
Craignish Bridge 79
Craigower 23-25, 27
Craigvinean Burn 51
Craigvinean Forest 64, 69, 73, 75
Craig y Barns 68, 75
Creag a' Chruidh 39
Creag an Fhithich 21
Creag Bhreac 19
Creag na h-Eighe 77
Creag na Uamha 10
Creegan, Rev. Christine 37
Culloden 87
Cumberland, Duke of 87

Deuchary Hill 16, 63
Douglas, David 68

Dowally Burn 76
Drummond Hill 93-95, 98
Drumochter Pass 20
Duchesses Bridal Path 59
Dull 85
Dunfallandy 38, 39
    Pictish stone 39
Dunkeld 19, 45-47, 51, 55, 59, 63,
    69, 71-73, 75
    Atholl Memorial Fountain 47
    Cathedral 47, 55, 59
    Ell Shop 47
    Heritage Trail 47
    Royal School 46
    Scottish Horse Regimental Museum
    47
Dunkeld House 59
Dunkeld House Hotel 59, 67
Dunmore, Earl of 23
Dunmore Loch 1, 2, 6
Dunmore Trail 23-25
Dunsinane 45, 57

Easterfield, Charlie 42
Edradour 27-29
    Distillery 27-29

Falls of Acharn 97-99
Falls of Bruar 105-107
Falls of the Braan 49-51, 69
Farragon Hill 35, 42, 79, 89, 93
Faskally House 2, 6
Faskally Wood 1, 6, 7
Fergusson, Mrs 23
floods 32, 76
Fonab Forest 33
Fonvuick 10, 13, 15
Forest Enterprise 41, 68
Forestry Commission 93
Freshwater Fisheries Research
    Laboratory 1, 6
Fungarth 71-73

Garry Bridge 2, 3
Garry footbridge 5
George II, King 83
Glack, The 63
Glen Garr 52
Glen Garry 15

Glen Girnaig 20
Glen Tilt 101-103
Gow, Niel 67
Graham of Claverhouse, John 2, 103
Grandtully 37, 85
Grant, Pat 11, 12
Grant, William 11

Haughend 71
Hay, Mrs Christian 11
Hermitage, The (Acharn) 98, 99
Hermitage, The (Dunkeld) 51, 68
hibernaculum 25
House of Bruar 105, 107

Inchewan Burn 55, 57
Inver 63
Isabella, Queen 43

Jacobite Risings 2, 3, 51, 87, 99

Kenmore 93, 99
Killiecrankie 1-3, 5, 6, 9, 11, 13, 19,
    24
    Battle of 2, 12, 103
Killiechangie 39
Kilmorich 77
King's Pass 60
King's Seat (Birnam Hill) 57
King's Seat (Dunkeld) 60, 61
Kirkmichael 63

Linn of Tummel 6, 7
Loch a' Choire 20
Loch Faskally 1, 5-7, 16, 31
Loch of the Lowes 57, 71, 72
Loch Tay 93-95, 97-99
Loch Tummel 24, 42
Logierait 37

MacBean, Donald 3
MacGregor, Rob Roy 3, 38, 59, 99
Mackenzie, Alexander 37, 43
Mann, Dennis 37
Marra, Michael 67
McGowan, Frank 47
McPherson, James 50
Menzies, Colonel 61
Menzies, Sir David 86
Menzies, Sir Neil 85

Menzies Monument 85
Middleton of Fonab 32
Mill Dam 63-65, 76
Mitchell, John 3, 12
Moness Burn and Falls 79-81
Moulin 19, 28, 29
Moulin Burn 19

National Trust for Scotland 2, 6, 9, 23, 47, 49, 68, 98
Netherton 32
Niel Gow's Oak 67

Old Military Roads 52, 81
Ossian's Cave 50
Ossian's Hall 49, 67, 69

Parent Larch 61
Pictish Road 35
Pitlochry 1, 5, 16, 23, 29, 31, 32, 35, 39
  Festival Theatre 31, 35
  Rotary Club 27
Polney Loch 60, 65, 75
Port-na-Craig 31
Potter, Beatrix 46

Queen's View 41, 43

Rannoch Moor 24
River Braan 49-51, 68
River Garry 1, 2, 6, 9, 13, 21
River Tay 32, 41, 46, 53, 58, 67-69, 76, 83-87, 94
River Tilt 103
River Tummel 6, 7, 31, 75
Robert the Bruce, King 43
Robin's Dam 56
Rohallion Lodge and Loch 56
Rotary Club of Pitlochry 27
Rotmell Farm 76
Rotmell Wood 64
Royal Society for the Protection of Birds 15-17
Rumbling Bridge 52

St Coed 37
St Colme's Well 60
St Cuthbert 86
St David's Well 86

Saltire Society 1
Schiehallion 21, 24, 42, 57, 90
Scottish Crannog Centre 99
Scottish Wildlife Trust 71, 72
Sgorr Clan Dhonnacaidh 10
Shakespeare, William 45
Shelloch Den 16
Shierglas Quarry 10
Sketewan 89
Society for the Propagation of Christian Knowledge 11
Soldier's Leap 3, 12
Stac an Fheidh 20
Stair Bridge 56
Stanley Hill 47, 61
Stewart, Miss (of Tenandry) 11
Strathtay 33

Tay Forest Park 41
Tay River Purification Board 31
Taymouth Castle 95
Telford, Thomas 45, 47
Tenandry 9-11
Tom na Cruiche 101
Tomgarrow 52
Torr an Eas 6
Tulliemet 77
Tummel Forest Park 21

Upper Hatton 63

Victoria, Queen 6, 21, 43, 102

Wade, General George 20, 83-85, 94
Wade's Bridge, Aberfeldy 83-87
Walker, Norman 12
Weem 83-87
Willie Miller's Well 76
Wisely, Captain 23
Wordsworth, William 106

Other titles in this series:

25 Walks: Arrochar, Cowal and Bute
25 Walks: Ayrshire and Arran
25 Walks: The Chilterns
25 Walks: The Cotswolds
25 Walks: Dumfries and Galloway
25 Walks: Edinburgh and Lothian
25 Walks: Fife
25 Walks: In and Around Belfast
25 Walks: In and Around Glasgow
25 Walks: In and Around London
25 Walks: In Down District
25 Walks: The Scottish Borders
25 Walks: Skye and Kintail
25 Walks: The Yorkshire Dales

Cycling Guides:

25 Cycle Routes: Argyll and Bute
25 Cycle Routes: In and Around Glasgow
25 Cycle Routes: The Kingdom of Fife

Also by Mercat Press:

Hill Walks: Glen Coe and Lochaber
The West Highland Way: Official Guide
The Southern Upland Way: Official Guide
St Cuthbert's Way: Official Guide